Strategic Human Resource Management in China

This book documents and explains how strategic human resource management (SHRM) and high performance work systems (HPWS) have been adopted among indigenous enterprises, namely state-owned enterprises (SOEs) and domestic private enterprises (DPEs) in China, from both management and employee perspectives.

The book examines the mutual relationships between employees and their supervisors/managers through social exchange theory. It explains how and why employees develop their perceptions and relationships with their immediate supervisors/managers in the working environment and the consequent effects on their attitudes and behaviour at work.

Given the importance of the Chinese economy in the world, and the impact of its 'open door' policy and economic and management reforms, this book will provide valuable insight into China's SHRM and HPWS.

Min Min recently graduated from the School of Management at the University of South Australia with a PhD thesis on 'Mediating mechanisms underlying strategic human resource management and high performance work system in China'. Before undertaking her PhD study, she completed her Bachelor and Master degrees in commerce at Macquarie University and had worked a number of years in Canberra as a professional accountant. Her teaching and research interests include strategic HRM, international HRM and comparative studies of HRM systems among emerging economies.

Mary Bambacas is Lecturer at the University of South Australia. Her work experience includes both profit and non-profit organizations and associations. She has held senior management positions in the public sector and the non-profit sector, as well as owning and managing a small business. Her interests lie with people management skills and organizational behaviour. Her work has been published in leading international journals including the *International Journal of Human Resource Management.*

Ying Zhu is Professor and Director of the Australian Centre for Asian Business at the University of South Australia. He has been working as a business leader as well as an academic leader in China and Australia for more than 30 years. He has published widely in the areas of international HRM, employment relations, labour law and regulations in Asia and economic development in Asia. His most recent authored monographs are *Managing Chinese Outward Foreign Direct Investment: From Entry Strategy to Sustainable Development in Australia* (Palgrave 2015) with Dr. Charlie Huang, *Teacher Management in China: The Transformation of Educational Systems* (Routledge 2016) with Dr. Eva Huang and Professor John Benson, *Business Leadership Development in China* (Routledge 2015) with Dr. Shuang Ren and Professor Robert Wood, *Law and Fair Work in China* (Routledge 2013) with Professors Sean Cooney and Sarah Biddulph and *The Everyday Impact of Economic Reform in China* (Routledge 2010) with Professors John Benson and Michael Webber.

Routledge Frontiers of Business Management

For a full list of titles in this series, please visit www.routledge.com/series/rfbm

1 **Managing Innovation and Cultural Management in the Digital Era**
The case of the National Palace Museum
Edited by Rua-Huan Tsaih and Tzu-Shian Han

2 **Managing Convergence in Innovation**
The new paradigm of technological innovation
Edited by Kong-rae Lee

3 **Corporate Sustainability Assessments**
Sustainability practices of multinational enterprises in Thailand
Edited by Jerome D. Donovan, Cheree Topple, Eryadi K. Masli and Teerin Vanichseni

4 **Knowledge Spillover-based Strategic Entrepreneurship**
Edited by João J. Ferreira, Leo-Paul Dana and Vanessa Ratten

5 **Japanese Management**
International perspectives
Hitoshi Iwashita

6 **Strategic Human Resource Management in China**
A Multiple Perspective
Min Min, Mary Bambacas and Ying Zhu

Strategic Human Resource Management in China

A Multiple Perspective

Min Min, Mary Bambacas and Ying Zhu

LONDON AND NEW YORK

First published 2017 by Routledge

2 Park Square, Milton Park, Abingdon, Oxfordshire OX14 4RN
52 Vanderbilt Avenue, New York, NY 10017

Routledge is an imprint of the Taylor & Francis Group, an informa business

First issued in paperback 2019

British Library Cataloguing-in-Publication Data
A catalogue record for this book is available from the British Library

Library of Congress Cataloging-in-Publication Data
A catalog record for this book has been requested

ISBN: 978-1-138-69065-3 (hbk)
ISBN: 978-0-367-37469-3 (pbk)

Typeset in Galliard
by Apex CoVantage, LLC

Contents

Figures

Tables

Preface

Employees can be identified as a source of competitive advantage. Strategic human resource management (SHRM) in general and high performance work systems (HPWS) in particular provide an efficient way for enterprises to utilize such an advantage, maintaining a lead in their industry. However, the definition of HPWS is ambiguous and is often considered to be a Western idea. The application and generalization of this idea in non-Western contexts remain underexplored. Additionally, SHRM/HPWS is traditionally treated as a management oriented approach, largely ignoring employees' roles and reactions. This book adopts the social exchange theory to explain employee attitudes in response to SHRM/HPWS initiated by their managers. In essence, it investigates the mediating effect of reciprocity and trust between HPWS and employee job satisfaction and turnover intention.

The research presented in this book consists of two separate, yet equally important studies. The first is an interview study, aimed at uncovering SHRM/HPWS practices implemented by management in both state-owned enterprises (SOEs) and domestic private enterprises (DPEs) in China, as well as analyzing employees' perceptions of these SHRM/HPWS practices and the effects of SHRM/HPWS on employee attitudes and behaviour. A total of 51 interviews were conducted; 40 full-time employees in a number of industries, such as transportation, manufacturing and software, and 11 senior HR managers were interviewed. The second study is a two-wave survey performed to examine the mediating role of employee-perceived trustworthiness of management in the workplace. Of the 1,196 survey questionnaires distributed, 956 were collected, reflecting an 80 percent response rate.

Stage One study (the interviews) found that there were differences between managers' choices and their implementation of SHRM/HPWS and employees' interpretations of SHRM/HPWS practices. Managers utilized these practices to signal to employees their concerns about performance improvement and business and developmental directions. Employees tended to perceive HR practices on the basis of whether these practices improved their skills, enhanced their participation and rewarded their contributions. The interview findings also illustrated that employee participation plays a positive role in the implementation of SHRM/HPWS. Employee participation, especially in decision-making processes, facilitates the establishment of mutual trust between employees and employers. It enhances the efficiency of communication between employees and management, which potentially aligns employees' interests with those of management.

Stage Two study (the survey) showed that there is a close relationship between the ways employees perceive HPWS specifically, the trust employees have in management and employee outcomes in both SOEs and DPEs. The findings indicated that employee perceptions of the HPWS implemented are positively related to their job satisfaction and negatively related to turnover intention. Furthermore, employees' trust in their supervisors/managers partially mediates the relationship between the HPWS and employee job satisfaction, as well as their turnover intention.

This research makes a contribution to the SHRM/HPWS literature. First, it targets employee perceptions of SHRM/HPWS and their effects on employee attitudes and behaviours. It approaches SHRM/HPWS and their effects at an individual level rather than at an organizational level. Second, employee outcomes arising from HPWS are treated in this research as employee responses to implemented HR practices. The findings also suggest that employee perceptions of and reactions to HR practices may be influenced by the perceptions and experiences of their supervisors/managers. Third, this research explores the possible mediating mechanism underlying HPWS, representing an effort to unlock the 'black box' between HPWS and employee outcomes. This research also makes a practical contribution by using the results of both studies to generate workplace practices that seek to increase employee participation and trust as a way of enhancing employee job satisfaction and reducing turnover intention.

The contributing authors in this volume are specialists in SHRM and HPWS studies in general and on Chinese HRM in particular. They have access to both the English and Chinese literature, to statistics and to government reports. This project received substantial support from the Australian Centre for Asian Business and the School of Management at the University of South Australia. We would also like to thank Marina Morgan for her support in the final proofreading. Finally, we are grateful for the support we have received from Routledge and for their willingness to publish on this important topic. We hope that this volume will create further interest in SHRM and HPWS in emerging economies and will provide the basis for a more comprehensive understanding of HRM among transitional emerging economies in the world.

Min Min, Mary Bambacas and Ying Zhu
July 2016

Abbreviations

AIC	Akaike information criterion
CFA	confirmatory factor analysis
CFI	comparative fit index
CPC	Communist Party of China
DPEs	domestic private enterprises
EFA	exploratory factor analysis
FIEs	foreign invested enterprises
HPWS	high performance work systems
HRM	human resource management
JVs	joint ventures
ML	maximum likelihood
MLM	maximum likelihood parameter estimates with standard errors and a mean-adjusted Chi-square test statistic
RMSEA	root mean square error of approximation
SEM	structural equation modelling
SHRM	strategic human resource management
SOEs	State-owned enterprises
SRMR	standardized root mean square residual
TLI	Tucker-Lewis Index

1 Introduction

Globalization, strategic HRM and China

Under the influence of globalization, organizations are facing challenges such as retaining sustained competitive advantage and differentiating themselves from their competitors. To cope with these challenges, human resource management (HRM) holds one of the keys to success. The new competitive reality requires new ways of thinking about HRM. Traditionally, HRM is defined as a set of processes and activities which are used jointly to solve people-related business problems. With the introduction of strategic human resource management (SHRM) theories, relevant policies and practices have made HR functions more supportive of business strategies by virtue of their transition from HRM to SHRM.

In the West, SHRM has gained credibility and popularity among researchers and HR professionals. These HR practices often take the Western rule as standard. However, when these same HR practices are implemented in a different environment, such as in Asia, replicating the Western model does not necessarily work (Gelfand et al., 2007). SHRM with 'Asian characteristics' is an emerging possibility (Zhu et al., 2007). China could be seen as a good example for investigating similarities and differences between Western and Eastern systems.

China has made attempts to reform its economy since the late 1970s. As economic reform proceeds, it is likely to match innovation in its management practices (Child, 1996). China has become the world's second largest economy and the largest exporter, surpassing the United States and Japan. Its unprecedented economic growth amazes both people in China and the rest of the world and increases concerns about the sustainability of the fast-paced economic growth. Simultaneously, the economic structure is undergoing change, shifting from an agricultural and industrial based economy towards the light manufacturing and service sectors (Wang and Wang, 2006). Industries such as health, education, finance, insurance, real estate, telecom and IT have seen significant growth while mining has experienced decline. In addition, these changes are related to the downsizing and privatizations of state-owned enterprises (SOEs), the introduction of performance management systems in the public sector, the growing strength of the private sector and the continuing pressure of unemployment (Cooke, 2012).

In SOEs, HR policies and practices are under state government control through regional and local personnel departments. The number of employees and payment levels are largely determined by governmental departments. It is common practice for managers to be merely involved in administrative functions and policy implementation (Child, 1996). Employees holding a job for life has been the norm (Warner, 1996). With the adoption of an 'open door' policy and commencement of economic reforms in the late 1970s, the dominance of SOEs started to weaken. SOEs have witnessed changes in HR policies and practices, such as a reduction of direct state control and the consequent increase of autonomy and responsibility at the enterprise level in major aspects of HR policies and practices (Child, 1996). Following the 'open door' policy and economic reforms, SOEs downsized, which led to a significant reduction in their number. Since the middle of the 1990s a large number of SOEs have been corporatized and privatized; nowadays only 110 centrally controlled SOEs and another 80,000 provincial and local government controlled SOEs remain (Cendrowski, 2015).

In parallel to these trends, the Chinese economy has been supplemented by the increasing role of domestic private enterprises (DPEs) and the competition brought by these enterprises (Warner and Zhu, 2010). The number of DPEs has soared to approximately 1,250,000 in China (China Private Enterprises Year Book, 2014). Unlike their SOE counterparts, DPEs are not strictly constrained by governmental control and historical heritage. They are considered to be more flexible, innovative and risk-taking (Wang et al., 2007). Therefore, it is meaningful to explore the HR practices and policies adopted and implemented in Chinese indigenous enterprises, namely SOEs and DPEs, given the growing diversity of business strategies and management practices in China.

These changes present a challenge to management in China in terms of coping strategies. Options include leaving management systems unchanged, developing new indigenous forms or adopting Western management systems. The choice made by management in China was to opt for a 'hybrid' approach using Western knowledge to implement an evolutionary change process within the Chinese context (Warner, 2013). This choice is meaningful and strategically oriented.

Besides the aforementioned macro-level changes, workforce changes are also significant. China makes up a substantial proportion of the world's population with a workforce that is increasingly educated and eager to succeed. It is common for people from different generations to work side by side. People of the same generation tend to be influenced by the same key historical and social life experiences of their era (Wey Smola et al., 2002). For example, millennials belong to a generation which has grown up with computers, the internet and social media, having a profound effect on the way they perceive and solve problems. They are encouraged to make their own decisions, challenge authority and value fairness. They desire a sense of belonging, the ability to learn, autonomy and feedback. They tend to be sceptical of the status quo and hierarchical relationships and expect managers to earn respect rather than gain respect by virtue of a title (Tulgan, 2004). Each generation has its own unique values, set of skills and characteristics (Gursoy et al., 2013), which creates challenges for management.

Most books have explored SHRM from a managerial perspective. The growing interest in this 'top-down' approach is easy to understand because HR policies and practices are traditionally implemented from a managerial perspective. Management is dominant during the decision-making process. However, the outcome of such decisions has significant impact on the life and well-being of employees. Given that there has been limited research in SHRM from a management and employee perspective, this book adopts a different approach to address this issue.

Discussion on management in general, and HRM in particular, cannot be isolated from the context. Given its importance in the global economy, China is a good example to be explored given the unique characteristics of its workforce and culture. Furthermore, this book focuses on Chinese indigenous enterprises (i.e., SOEs and DPEs). Both enterprises have witnessed dramatic changes during the economic reformation in terms of political power, size, numbers and organizational structure. They have been influenced by the Western management theory introduced by direct foreign investment, management programs and education systems such as the MBA (Warner, 2004). At the same time, they maintain and demonstrate their own features in HRM. Therefore, understanding which HRM system is adopted, discovering how this system is implemented and finding a possible explanation of how this system works in these indigenous enterprises is very meaningful.

Research framework

Most SHRM studies focus on Western advanced economies such as the US, UK, Germany, Finland, Australia and New Zealand (Boselie et al., 2001, Guthrie, 2001, Guest et al., 2003, Heffernan and Dundon, 2016). Similar studies in China are sparse. Given the importance of the Chinese economy in the world and the impact of its 'open door' policy and economic and management reforms, it is meaningful to develop SHRM research in China.

This book discusses SHRM in general and high performance work systems (HPWS) in particular. HPWS is a set of mutually reinforcing key SHRM practices that select, develop, retain and motivate employees to achieve superior performance. Prior research has primarily focused on managerial reports on using HPWS (Lepak et al., 2006), ignoring the role of individual employees' actual perceptions of these systems (Boon et al., 2011).

Placing employees at the centre of a SHRM/HPWS study is meaningful. HPWS practices have an important signalling effect to employees (Wayne et al., 2002). Employees understand organizational objectives and expectations by interpreting the HR policies and practices adopted (Bowen and Ostroff, 2004). Employees observe and interact with their immediate supervisors/managers during the implementation of SHRM/HPWS. The way they perceive the intentions and attitudes of their immediate supervisors/managers (Whitener, 2001) influences their attitude towards work and their behaviour (Dittrich and Carrell, 1979). In addition, ordinate employees constitute a large proportion of the workforce in enterprises. Given the number and variety of ordinate employees, exploring SHRM/HPWS from their perspectives enhances the generalization and practical applicability of this book.

Another key aspect of this book is the mutual relationship between employees and their supervisors/managers. Social exchange theory (Blau, 1964) has been chosen as one of the key underpinning theories in this book. This theory involves a series of interactions that generate obligations among people. These interactions could be seen as interdependent on the actions of another person, which has the potential to generate high quality relationships (Emerson, 1976) such as mutual trust. By adopting the social exchange theory, we explain how and why employees develop perceptions of and relationships with their immediate supervisors/managers in the working environment and explore the subsequent effects these have on their attitudes and behaviour at work.

Therefore, this book aims:

1 To identify the SHRM/HPWS practices implemented in SOEs and DPEs. This is achieved by targeting managers from sampled companies in China. Their responses contain rich information on managerial intention, procedures and expected outcomes of SHRM/HPWS practices adopted in their companies.
2 To explore the mediating effect of trust relationships between supervisors/managers and employees on the implementation of SHRM/HPWS. This will be achieved by analysing employees' responses and developing a conceptual framework, incorporating factors proposed from existing literature and the findings from employee interviews.
3 To explore additional context-specific insights into the adoption and implementation of SHRM/HPWS in Chinese indigenous enterprises by evaluating managers' and employees' responses, as well as other unique issues and characteristics affecting SHRM/HPWS implementation. This can offer new insights into issues that have not been covered in existing literature. Moreover, the adopted SHRM/HPWS assists managers in improving their management functions by involving employees in the decision-making process.

In order to tackle these objectives, there are four questions we address based on the research carried out in this book:

- What are the SHRM/HPWS adopted and implemented in China from manager and employee perspectives?
- What insights can we gain about SHRM and HPWS in SOEs and DPEs in China?
- What HRM systems can organizations develop to encourage positive attitudes and intentions to stay?
- What direction should managers and organizations take in implementing strategies for HRM and HPWS?

Summary of research methods

This research adopts a mixed-method design which has been increasingly established as a legitimate methodological choice and is utilized in social science.

Although mixed-method designs are strongly advocated, genuinely mixed-method designs which triangulate findings from qualitative and quantitative studies remain sparse. In this book, a qualitative study was first adopted to provide researchers with opportunities to understand the same HR issues from different angles within the same context. A quantitative survey was then performed to test certain meaningful factors found in the qualitative study. A combination of qualitative and quantitative approaches through a mixed-method design provides researchers with the flexibility to explore uncertain issues regarding the impact of cultural, societal and institutional factors. This research lends support to conducting mixed-method studies in the field of SHRM/HPWS in the context of China in transition (see Figure 1.1).

Stage One of the study aimed to confirm the adoption and implementation of SHRM/HPWS and to identify any unknown issues. By performing

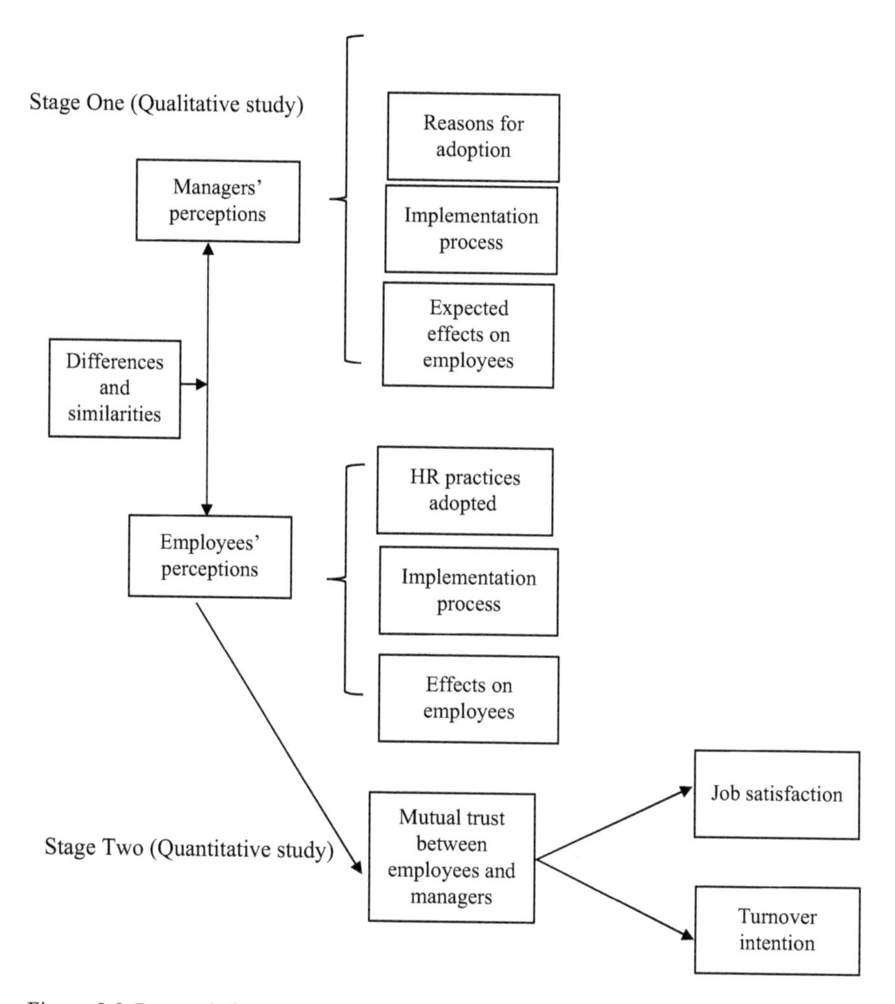

Figure 1.1 Research framework

semi-structured interviews, this first stage provided details and explorative data to understand the SHRM/HPWS practices being adopted and implemented in selected companies, and how these HR practices are implemented to achieve the companies' goals, as well as how these HR practices influence employee attitudes and behaviour at work. The interviewees comprised 11 managers and 40 employees. A comprehensive view of the relevant issues was obtained by combining responses from both managers and employees, while a comparison of these responses helped identify differences and similarities between managers' and employees' perceptions.

Stage Two of the study is a two-wave survey study that was conducted in SOEs and DPEs across four locations in China. The survey was developed based on extensive literature reviews and findings from interviews. It intended to evaluate employees' perceptions of SHRM/HPWS implemented in their companies, perceived trustworthiness, job satisfaction and turnover intention. The survey study helped generalize findings and further identify relationships across a large sample. A total of 907 valid questionnaires were collected from 245 employees in SOEs and 662 employees in DPEs.

In the data analysis process, structural equation modelling (SEM) techniques were adopted for data analysis. Due to little empirical evidence related to SHRM/HPWS studies in China, an exploratory factor analysis (EFA) was firstly utilized to determine an appropriate number of factors and the pattern of factor loadings from the data. A confirmatory factor analysis (CFA) was then performed to test the measurement model and structure model.

Outline of the book

The book contains a total of six chapters. Chapter 1 provides the rationale for SHRM/HPWS research in Chinese indigenous companies. Research gaps and aims are discussed. A brief research method description is presented.

Following the introductory chapter, chapter 2 reviews the evolution of the literature from HRM to SHRM. Subsequently, the focus shifts to HPWS literature by examining the importance of employee perceptions and participation elements. The chapter then reviews social exchange theory, which underpins this research. By applying social exchange theory to HPWS, this chapter provides a theoretical framework explaining the creation of a mutual investment-based relationship between employees and their supervisors/managers. Lastly, this chapter presents HPWS studies which examine the systems' effects on organizational performance and employee outcomes.

Building on the previous chapter, chapter 3 presents the overall studies on SHRM/HPWS in China and then establishes the appropriate research methods and data analysis. It introduces the mixed-method approach and addresses issues related to the rationale of the research design.

Chapter 4 illustrates similarities and differences in the adoption and implementation of SHRM/HPWS in SOEs and DPEs. The characteristics embedded in these two types of ownership affect how managers design and implement

HR policies and practices. Without constraints from governmental departments, DPEs enjoy a relatively high level of flexibility during implementation. As to SOEs, they are sufficiently funded, which enables them to train employees well. A comparison is also performed between managers and employees. By looking into their responses, the results reveal that employees' interpretations of HR policies and practices are not always consistent with those intended by managers. Such inconsistency further urges a need for employees' involvement during the process of adoption and implementation.

Chapter 5 begins with an explanation of the employees' survey and their perception of and participation in the adoption and development of HPWS. In addition to interviews, the statistical analysis lends support to our understanding of trust as the mediating mechanism underlying the HPWS–outcome relationship. In this chapter, a number of hypotheses regarding employees' perceptions and their participation in HPWS, the impact of HPWS on their job satisfaction and turnover intention and the mediating effect of trust relationships between employees and their supervisors/managers are tested.

Chapter 6 triangulates findings from both qualitative and quantitative studies. Based on the triangulation, the chapter draws a relatively comprehensive picture of the adoption and implementation of SHRM/HPWS. A SHRM/HPWS with 'Chinese characteristics' is revealed, illustrating that this system is adopted critically. This chapter also develops a better understanding of how SHRM/HPWS influences employees in Chinese indigenous enterprises. Combining managers' and employees' perceptions of the same issues provides a way beyond the traditional, and approaches the issues solely from managers' perceptions. Moreover, this chapter also presents the theoretical and methodological contributions, as well as the practical implications, of this research. It is followed by concluding remarks which elaborate on the limitations of the research and future research directions.

References

Blau, P. M. 1964. *Exchange and power in social life*, Piscataway, NJ: Transaction Publishers.

Boon, C., Den Hartog, D. N., Boselie, P. and Paauwe, J. 2011. The relationship between perceptions of HR practices and employee outcomes: Examining the role of person–organisation and person–job fit. *The International Journal of Human Resource Management*, 22, 138–162.

Boselie, P., Paauwe, J. and Jansen, P. 2001. Human resource management and performance: Lessons from the Netherlands. *International Journal of Human Resource Management*, 12, 1107–1125.

Bowen, D. E. and Ostroff, C. 2004. Understanding HRM–firm performance linkages: The role of the 'strength' of the HRM system. *Academy of Management Review*, 29, 203–221.

Cendrowski, S. 2015. *Why China's SOE reform would always disappoint* [Online]. Available: http://fortune.com/2015/09/15/why-chinas-soe-reform-would-always-disappoint/ [Accessed March 12 2016].

Child, J. 1996. *Management in China during the age of reform*, Cambridge: Cambridge University Press.

China Private Enterprises Year Book 2014. *China private enterprises year book*, Beijing: All-China Federation of Industry and Commerce Press.

Cooke, F. L. 2012. *Human resource management in China new trends and practices*, Abingdon, Oxon: New York: Routledge.

Dittrich, J. E. and Carrell, M. R. 1979. Organizational equity perceptions, employee job satisfaction, and departmental absence and turnover rates. *Organizational Behavior and Human Performance*, 24, 29–40.

Emerson, R. M. 1976. Social exchange theory. *Annual Review of Sociology*, 2, 335–362.

Gelfand, M. J., Erez, M. and Aycan, Z. 2007. Cross-cultural organizational behavior. *Annual Review of Psychology*, 58, 479–514.

Guest, D. E., Michie, J., Conway, N. and Sheehan, M. 2003. Human resource management and corporate performance in the UK. *British Journal of Industrial Relations*, 41, 291–314.

Gursoy, D., Chi, C. G.-Q. and Karadag, E. 2013. Generational differences in work values and attitudes among frontline and service contact employees. *International Journal of Hospitality Management*, 32, 40–48.

Guthrie, J. P. 2001. High-involvement work practices, turnover, and productivity: Evidence from New Zealand. *Academy of Management Journal*, 44, 180–190.

Heffernan, M. and Dundon, T. 2016. Cross-level effects of high-performance work systems (HPWS) and employee well-being: The mediating effect of organisational justice. *Human Resource Management Journal*, 26, 211–231.

Lepak, D. P., Liao, H., Chung, Y. and Harden, E. E. 2006. A conceptual review of human resource management systems in strategic human resource management research. *Research in Personnel and Human Resources Management*, 25, 217–271.

Tulgan, B. 2004. Trends point to a dramatic generational shift in the future workforce. *Employment Relations Today*, 30, 23–31.

Wang, J. and Wang, G. G. 2006. Exploring national human resource development: A case of China management development in a transitioning context. *Human Resource Development Review*, 5, 176–201.

Wang, X., Bruning, N. S. and Peng, S. 2007. Western high-performance HR practices in China: A comparison among public-owned, private and foreign-invested enterprises. *The International Journal of Human Resource Management*, 18, 684–701.

Warner, M. 1996. Human resources in the people's republic of China: The 'Three Systems' reforms. *Human Resource Management Journal*, 6, 32–43.

Warner, M. 2004. Human resource management in China revisited: Introduction. *The International Journal of Human Resource Management*, 15, 617–634.

Warner, M. 2013. *Human resource management 'with Chinese characteristics': Facing the challenges of globalization*, London: Routledge.

Warner, M. and Zhu, Y. 2010. Labour and management in the people's Republic of China: Seeking the 'harmonious society'. *Asia Pacific Business Review*, 16, 285–298.

Wayne, S. J., Shore, L. M., Bommer, W. H. and Tetrick, L. E. 2002. The role of fair treatment and rewards in perceptions of organizational support and leader-member exchange. *Journal of Applied Psychology*, 87, 590–598.

Wey Smola, K., Sutton, C. D. and Gephart, R. P. 2002. Generational differences: Revisiting generational work values for the new millennium. *Journal of Organizational Behavior*, 23, 363–382.

Whitener, E. M. 2001. Do 'high commitment' human resource practices affect employee commitment? A cross-level analysis using hierarchical linear modeling. *Journal of Management*, 27, 515–535.

Zhu, Y., Warner, M. and Rowley, C. 2007. Human resource management with 'Asian' characteristics: A hybrid people-management system in East Asia. *The International Journal of Human Resource Management*, 18, 745–768.

2 Evolution of SHRM/ HPWS and social exchange theory

Introduction

Over the past decades, research on comprehensive understandings of HRM has moved beyond traditional administrative responsibilities and is recognized as contributing to organizational effectiveness. With the introduction of SHRM theories, policies and practices, HR functions are more supportive of organizational strategies and aim to enhance the realization of organizational goals. In addition to this tendency, a substantial number of SHRM research projects have emerged, investigating the direct relationship between HR practices and organizational performance outcomes such as financial performance and organizational effectiveness (Batt, 2002; Datta et al., 2005; Wright et al., 2005). Since SHRM initially focuses on the relationship between HR practices and organizational performance, it largely promotes the interests of the organization with less attention on employees' interests, voice and well-being.

In recent years, SHRM studies have been extended to include the individual employee perspective with a focus on HPWS, including employee participation, job satisfaction, commitment and organizational citizenship behaviour (Allen et al., 2003; Kuvaas, 2008; Snape and Redman, 2010). The benefits of placing employees at the centre of SHRM/HPWS studies are two-fold. First, employees are directly affected by HR policies and practices. Understanding employees' perceptions of HR policies and practices provides a path with which to explore how these policies and practices work effectively. Secondly, conventional SHRM studies focus primarily on the management perspective, which can lead to increased bias. By including employees with an emphasis on HPWS through employees' participation, studies help provide a comprehensive picture from multiple viewpoints. It is important to learn whether employees can proactively participate in the formation and implementation of HR practices – this is the key contribution the present book wishes to make.

Social exchange theory has been chosen in this book as one of the key theoretical underpinnings. It provides a solid theoretical framework to explain how and why employees develop exchange relationships with organizations and immediate supervisors. It also provides a rationale for explaining how employee perceptions are related to relationship building and influence performance and satisfaction in the workplace.

Trust is a positive relational construct in social exchange relationships. Interactions between people can generate high quality exchanges such as trust. Trust is a set of confident beliefs in someone else in organizational settings and an indispensable component in understanding relational exchanges between employees and their supervisors. Feelings of trustworthiness towards management are associated with HR practices. The way HR practices are implemented influences employees' perceptions of being valued and respected, which leads to feelings of attachment to the organization.

This chapter reviews the evolution of the literature from HRM to SHRM. Subsequently, the focus shifts to HPWS literature and examines the importance of employee perceptions and participation during HPWS implementation. Social exchange theory, which underpins this study, is also reviewed. Lastly, this chapter describes HPWS studies on trust, followed by studies that examine the effects of HR practices on employee outcomes. In applying social exchange theory to SHRM studies, HR practices adopted by managers are interpreted by employees as 'signals' of managers' intentions (Den Hartog et al., 2004). Employees form perceptions of management's intentions and attitudes according to the way these HR practices are implemented. Of course, interpretation of HR practices varies according to factors such as previous experiences employees have had of these practices, differences in employment status, employment preferences and relationships with supervisors. By examining employees' perceptions and their actual experiences of HR practices, a conceptual framework and hypotheses are developed and linked to employee outcomes.

'Hard' and 'soft' HRM models

The two distinct models of 'hard' and 'soft' HRM can be traced back to the US (Storey, 2007). The hard HRM model, also termed the 'instrumental approach', focuses on employees as resources. They are considered to be assets or commodities of organizations under the control of management (Roan et al., 2001). Within the hard HRM model, employees are a passive production factor and a tool to be utilized by the organization (Storey, 2007). From a management perspective, the cost of labour is to be minimized with limited training, benefits and wages (Druker et al., 1996). Soft HRM, also known as the 'developmental humanist' approach, advocates that organizational performance can be achieved by winning employees' commitment instead of controlling employees (Legge, 2005). It is rooted in human relations and emphasizes communication, training and development, motivation, culture, values and employee involvement (Storey, 2007) and offers extensive skills training, benefits and high wages.

In reality, these two models are generally implemented by incorporating both concepts instead of being applied in their pure forms (Storey, 1992). In the pursuit of efficiency, management tends to adopt the hard model (Legge, 2005), while the soft model tends to be used in the form of job enrichment and multi-skilling (Legge, 2005; Roan et al., 2001).

Comparing these two models, it is easy to spot that the hard model 'controls' employees and utilizes employees efficiently and effectively as a production input.

Alternatively, the soft model recognizes the importance of employee commitment. Winning employee commitment is positively related to enhanced performance. Such control versus commitment is widely accepted (Walton, 1985). Additionally, neither HRM model takes into account the role of business strategy; therefore, more recently, the focus has shifted from general HRM approaches towards SHRM approaches. The following section presents a more detailed illustration.

From HRM to SHRM: a systems-level approach

Since the 1990s, organizations have increasingly become enamoured with the concept of SHRM, which aims to develop and maintain an organization's strategic infrastructure. Compared to HRM, SHRM is an area which has a more macro-orientation and has gradually recognized the importance of integration (Butler, 1991). SHRM emphasizes the entire HRM system, instead of focusing on individual HR policies or practices (Becker et al., 1997). HR practices in the strategic approach are linked to organizational business and strategic initiatives; they cohere across policy areas and across hierarchies, and they are accepted and used by line managers as part of their everyday work (Guest and Grant, 1991).

Four approaches in SHRM

The existence of a set of universally effective HR practices is one of the topics debated continually in SHRM studies. Initially, a set of HR practices, referred to as 'best practices', was proposed by Pfeffer (1994): employment security, selective hiring, decentralization and team self-management, high compensation based on performance, extensive training, reduced status differentiations and information sharing. The 'best practice' approach has been shown to work, from low technology applications to high technology manufacturing processes (Arthur, 1994). Pfeffer (1994) suggested that the more a company's HR system was similar to an ideal HR system, the more likely the company would be to outperform its competitors.

'Best practice' implies a universal applicability of HR practices; in other words, these practices can be easily imitated by competitors. A company implements a set of HR practices, hoping for increased performance and competitive advantage. If such a set of HR practices is simultaneously duplicated by others, a competitive advantage is not sustained (Barney, 1991); therefore, the 'best practices' approach is contradicted by the inimitability of sustained competitive advantage which might not be favoured by management.

An alternative approach to 'best practices' is the 'best fit' approach. It consists of two types of fit, horizontal fit and vertical fit. Horizontal fit means internal consistency of HR policies and practices, while vertical fit refers to congruence of the HR system with organizational strategy (Delery, 1998; Delery and Doty, 1996). Horizontal fit advocates that individual practices cannot be effectively implemented in isolation; it is important to put them into bundles with other practices to enhance organizational effectiveness (Guthrie et al., 2009). Horizontal fit is regarded as instrumental for efficiently managing human resources (Wright and Snell, 1998). The vertical alignment addresses an explicit alignment between HR practices and business strategy (Delery and Doty, 1996). Successfully linking organizational strategies with HR practices can enhance organizational performance (Posthuma et al., 2013). Therefore, the 'best fit' approach emphasizes that HR practices should link to business and other strategies to achieve business goals (Wright and McMahan, 1992). Empirical studies have supported this notion that superior performance can be achieved by combining such strategic fit, horizontally and vertically (Delery and Doty, 1996; Park et al., 2005).

The third approach linking SHRM practices and firm performance is the resource-based view. Employee skills, knowledge and abilities are seen as resources (Wright et al., 1994), and capitalizing on such resources has been proposed as a means of gaining competitive advantage (Schuler and MacMillan, 1984). This competitive advantage is sustained when a firm implements a value-creating strategy which is not simultaneously being implemented by current or potential competitors (Barney, 1991). Drawing from the logic of the resource-based view, organizations adopt SHRM practices to create and maintain valuable and inimitable human capital, which drives high organizational performance (Delery and Shaw, 2001; Ployhart and Moliterno, 2011).

Finally, the behavioural perspective is widely discussed and used in the SHRM literature (Schuler, 1991). It is described by Schuler and Jackson (1987) as the approach used to determine what is needed from employees apart from specific technical skills, knowledge and abilities required to perform a specific task. The assumption is that the purpose of HR practices is to elicit employee attitudes and behaviours. According to this perspective, organizations adopt HR practices to encourage productive behaviours from employees and thus achieve desirable operational and financial outcomes (Becker et al., 1998). Specifically, different aspects of organizations, such as business strategy, affect employee attitudes and behaviours preferred in the workplace. If an organization requires efficiency, its choice of HR practices is likely to differ from that of an organization that expects employees to be cooperative. According to the behavioural perspective approach, the effectiveness of HR practices is realized when employees act in ways that are needed for implementing strategies and achieving various business objectives. This model prioritizes the role of employee behaviour, instead of knowledge, skills and abilities.

In summary, each of the four approaches emphasizes different facets of SHRM. The 'best practices' approach explores a set of SHRM practices which is expected to be universally applicable. The 'best fit' approach addresses the role of alignment: alignment between practices, as well as between practices and business strategy. The bundle of practices is the unit of analysis rather than individual practices. The resource-based view examines SHRM using employees' skills, knowledge and abilities as the source of competitive advantage. SHRM is adopted to create and maintain unique human capital and subsequently boosts organizational performance. The behavioural perspective encourages positive employee attitudes and behaviours. In this approach, organizational performance is enhanced by affecting employee attitudes and encouraging employees to behave as expected.

High performance work systems

HPWS are a set of SHRM practices which emphasize direct employee involvement in the process of implementing SHRM. The concept offers opportunities for employees to be involved, either directly through teamwork, flexible job descriptions and idea-capturing schemes or indirectly through information dissemination or training specifically (Lawler III, 1986).

Among SHRM studies, no consistent agreement has been reached on the constituents of HPWS (Becker and Gerhart, 1996). It is generally suggested that these systems should include rigorous and selective staffing, extensive training and development, incentive compensation and merit-based performance appraisal (Lepak et al., 2006; Selden et al., 2013). Regardless of which HR practices are suggested to be included, employee participation/involvement is seen as one of the crucial elements of HPWS (Lawler, 1986). The importance of employee participation/involvement is repeatedly addressed in the relevant studies. Appelbaum (2000) associated 'opportunity to participate' with key high involvement mechanisms such as self-directed teams and quality circles. Macky and Boxall (2008) also suggested that the key mechanism in HPWS was employee participation, which affects performance through 'greater discretionary effort from employees'. According to Posthuma et al. (2013), HPWS aim to enhance organizational performance and to achieve a competitive advantage by improving employee motivation, participation, involvement and commitment.

Employee participation

Employees can participate through different schemes. Employee voice is one of the participation schemes (Mowbray et al., 2015) and is defined as the expression of an individual's opinions on decision-making (Thibaut and Walker, 1975) and as an expression of job dissatisfaction (Milliken et al., 2003). Both definitions of employee voice consider it to be the employees' expression of grievances, dissatisfaction, demands for change and reactions to management's plans and initiatives. Employee voice is an appropriate element through which to examine the impact on employee attitudes and behaviours (Gao et al., 2011). It positively affects employee perceptions of fairness and behavioural output (Greenberg, 1990; Tyler, 1986); for instance, making comments and speaking up improve organizational performance (Morrison and Milliken, 2000); employee voice decreases involuntary turnover (Burris et al., 2013). In addition, HR systems that do not include procedures encouraging employees to voice their views may be associated with negative outcomes (Knoll and Redman, 2015; Shaw et al., 2009; Yijing and Yong, 2015).

Information sharing is another way of involving employees. It is considered an important feature of employee participation in which employees receive autonomy and responsibility (Scott et al., 2003). Information sharing enhances employees' understanding of the organization's objectives and their own role in the achievement of these goals. Employees prefer to work for organizations where they can speak up and share their thoughts openly (Milliken et al., 2003; Zhou and George, 2001). With enhanced understanding, employees tend to perceive their jobs to be more secure and their career prospects to be better. Employees who have received information from their managers are more likely to participate and to make constructive suggestions. In this sense, information sharing facilitates a formal flow of communication among employees (Ling and Kellermanns, 2010). The existence of information sharing has been demonstrated to facilitate building trust between employees and their managers (Gao et al., 2011) and increases the level of work engagement and learning goal orientation (Maden, 2015).

Employee empowerment enhances flexibility and promptness by directing decision-making towards individuals (Kanter and Stein, 1979). It is a way of involving employees in a decision-making process in which they rarely participate. When a working environment is structured in such a way that employees feel empowered, employee attitudes are affected, which can lead to increased organizational efficiency (Fernandez and Moldogaziev, 2011). Empowerment can be facilitated by job characteristics, receiving support and opportunities to learn and develop. Mutual support between supervisors and colleagues further influences the empowerment of employees. Subsequently, employees are affected by such empowerment and tend to be more productive and successful in meeting organizational goals. Studies have shown that empowering employees positively affects individual employee outcomes such as job satisfaction (Bowen and Lawler, 1992; Davies et al., 2006; Fulford and Enz, 1995; Kim, 2002; Lee et al., 2006; Liden et al., 2000; Savery and Luks, 2001; Wright and Kim, 2004), commitment (Bhatnagar, 2007; Elloy, 2012; Raub and Robert, 2013) and performance (Fernandez and Moldogaziev, 2013)

To sum up, HPWS are a set of HR practices that advocate employee participation (Lawler, 1986). The invitation to be more involved is a signal to the employees that they are respected and that their contributions are recognized by their employers. Being able to directly voice their opinions, being informed of the organization's objectives and being empowered to make decisions increases the level of employee participation. These schemes of employee participation build trust between employees and managers (Barraud-Didier et al., 2012; Kim et al., 2013; Krosgaard et al., 2002).

Although the importance of employee participation has been recognized by HPWS studies, employee participation approaches are mainly explored from manager perspectives. Employees are invited to participate, which implies that employees remain passive recipients. Therefore, it is important to know whether employees can proactively participate in the formation and implementation of

HPWS. By conducting this research with an employee-centric approach, some light is expected to be shed on these issues.

Employee-centric HR studies

Links between HR practices and performance have been extensively explored. A growing body of evidence has demonstrated the positive outcomes resulting from HPWS – for example, organizational financial performance (Bae and Lawler, 2000; Evans and Davis, 2005), operational performance (Guthrie, 2001; Ichniowski and Shaw, 1999), occupational safety (Zacharatos et al., 2005), improved organizational effectiveness (Bartram et al., 2007) and higher motivation and commitment levels among workers (Gould-Williams, 2003; Whitener, 2001). The majority of studies have examined management initiatives in adopting HPWS (Armstrong et al., 2010; Lawler et al., 2011). Less attention has been given to the role and reaction of employees in HR studies (Guest, 2002).

Criticism regarding the neglect of employees in mainstream HR studies is directed at management. Managers often set the efficient exploitation of employee skills and knowledge as their top priority rather than acting in partnership with employees (Kochan and Osterman, 1995). Employee commitment is ignored during the implementation of strategies. Moreover, DeConinck (2010) pointed out that research from management perspectives could lead to self-reporting based on management's own interests, which can lead to increased bias (Guest, 2002). Likewise, Wright and Boswell (2002) stated that many of the studies focused primarily on management perspectives of the HR practices generally implemented with regard to all of the employees in an organization. Few studies have examined the HPWS targeted at different employee groups, and even fewer have examined the HPWS actually experienced by individual employees. Therefore, this study attempts to draw attention to employees, and their perceptions, experiences, attitudes and behaviour at work, in order to make complementary contributions towards the current literature.

According to Guest (2002), there are two ways of including employees in HPWS studies – one is to focus on employee outcomes, and the other is to incorporate them into the HPWS–performance linkage. By doing this, positive associations between HR practices and performance are expected to partially depend on employee responses to their experience of HR practices; in other words, employee perspectives of HPWS can be a key factor in understanding the HPWS–performance relationship.

Few studies have explicitly incorporated employee responses and perspectives. Appelbaum (2000) tested the effects of HPWS on employee trust, job satisfaction, job stress and commitment. Key HR practices were chosen, including autonomy in decision-making, communication with people, training and development for skill enhancement and membership of teams. These practices provided employees with opportunities to participate, which positively impacted employee outcomes. Another study (Ramsay et al., 2000) reported an association between HPWS and management-rated workplace performance, as well as the relationship between the same set of practices and employee-reported outcomes (i.e., commitment, pay satisfaction, employee-management relations, perceived job security and perceived job strain). Using the same data from Ramsay and colleagues' study, Guest (2001) analyzed the results at the organizational level rather than the individual level. They suggested a mediating effect of employee attitudes and behaviour in the HPWS–performance relationship. Den Hartog et al. (2013) also investigated the mediating role of employee-rated HR practices in the link between manager-rated HR practices and perceived unit performance. Kehoe and Wright (2013) further tested the mediating role of affective commitment between HPWS and organizational citizenship behaviour of employees, employee intention to stay with the organization and absenteeism. Boon et al. (2014) analyzed relationship between HPWS and employee absenteeism based on employee satisfaction and willingness to exert extra effort. Cafferkey and Dundon (2015) tested the relationship between HPWS and employee outcomes (i.e., job satisfaction, commitment, motivation and discretionary efforts) using organizational climate as a mediating factor. García-Chas et al. (2016) demonstrated that HPWS increases job satisfaction through employee-perceived organizational support, and Elorza et al. (2016) investigated the mediating role of employee-rated HPWS between management-rated HPWS and individual discretionary behaviour.

The combined findings of these studies indicate an increasing tendency to include employee perceptions and attitudes in HPWS studies. Placing employees at the centre of the study helps researchers understand how HPWS work effectively. Employee perceptions affect the implementation of HR policies and practices. Furthermore, the realization of effective HPWS needs the interaction, mutual trust and on-going social exchange engagements between employees and managers.

Social exchange theory

Social exchange theory involves a series of interactions that generate obligations among people. These interactions are seen as dependent on the actions of another person and have the potential to generate high quality relationships (Emerson, 1976). The theory entails unspecified obligations; when one person does another a favour, there is an expectation of some future return, although exactly when it will occur and in what form is not clear (Gouldner, 1960). In employment relationships, social exchange theory recognizes that employees prefer to take a long-term approach to social exchange relationships at work, with the pattern of reciprocity over time (Blau, 1964; Rousseau, 1989). Employees can form distinguishable social exchange relationships with their immediate supervisors (Liden et al., 1997; Wang et al., 2015), co-workers (Ensher et al., 2001; Farmer et al., 2015; Flynn, 2003), organizations (Ertürk and Vurgun, 2015; Golden and Veiga, 2015; Moorman et al., 1998), customers (Sheth, 1996) and suppliers (McEvily et al., 2003).

Perceived organizational support

Perceived organizational support is used to explain the development of employee commitment to an organization, which entails employees developing global beliefs concerning the extent to which the organization values their contributions and cares about their well-being (Eisenberger et al., 2001). In other words, employees appreciate their organization's commitment to them, which in turn contributes to employees' commitment to their organizations. High levels of perceived organizational support create feelings of obligation, where employees feel that they ought to be committed to their employers and feel obligated to reciprocate organizational support by engaging in behaviours that support organizational goals. That is, employees seek a balance in their exchange relationships with organizations by adopting attitudes and behaviours in response to the degree of organizational support given to them as individuals. Studies have shown that perceived organizational support is positively related to employee commitment and the fulfilment of responsibilities (Eisenberger et al., 2014). Empirical studies have also established a direct relationship between employee perceptions of being valued and increased employee trust towards managers (Ambrose and Schminke, 2003; Aselage and Eisenberger, 2003; DeConinck, 2010; Gordon et al., 2014).

Leader-member exchange

Leader-member exchange suggests that an interpersonal relationship evolves between supervisors and subordinates. Leaders convey role expectations to their employees and provide rewards to those employees who satisfy these expectations. Likewise, employees hold role expectations of their leaders on how their leaders are to treat and reward them (Gordon et al., 2014; Wang et al., 2005). This situation provides a basis of exchange between employees and supervisors (Wayne et al., 1997). In this exchange process, each party offers something the other party sees as valuable, and each party sees the exchange as reasonably equitable or fair (Graen and Scandura, 1987). The quality of the relationships is closely related to job performance. Allocating standard benefits in return for standard job performance is perceived as a low quality exchange (Wang et al., 2005). In high quality leader-member exchange relationships, social exchange is nourished by mutual trust, respect and obligations (Graen and Uhl-Bien, 1995). Favourable treatment by leaders impacts positively on respect, loyalty and obligation and consequently performance contribution (e.g., volunteering to work extra hours to meet deadlines and placing collective interests over short-term personal gratification).

These two relational exchanges are conceptualized at different levels. Perceived organizational support is conceptualized as the social exchanges taking place between an employee and the employer in general, while the leader-member exchange is viewed as the exchange relationship that takes place between an employee and a supervisor (Settoon et al., 1996). Perceived organizational support is found to predict organizational commitment, but not job performance. Leader-member exchange is claimed to predict performance and employee actions beneficial to supervisors (Settoon et al., 1996).

Moreover, these two relational exchanges exert effects on each other. To be specific, the quality of leader-member exchanges appears to have a stronger effect on perceived organizational support, affecting employee perceptions of organizational support. Leaders (managers) are perceived by members (employees) as those who are responsible for making influential decisions at work, such as promotions, salary increases, training, career advice and networking information (Sparrowe and Liden, 1997). They are also perceived as representative of organizations, who transmit business strategies and policies to employees. Such expansion of information leads to increased perceived support (Burt, 1992). Therefore, the exchange between leaders and their subordinates facilitates perceived organizational support (Eisenberger et al., 2001), which, in turn, affects the quality of exchange between employees and their managers. On the one hand, managers develop higher expectations of employees who are supported by the organization. On the other hand, employees can improve their level of skills and abilities by receiving strong organizational support. Possession of skills and abilities is valued by their managers in return (Wayne et al., 1997).

Social exchange theory and employee perceptions in HPWS studies

Employees form perceptions about management's intentions and attitudes towards them by interpreting HPWS practices and policies enacted by the organization (Whitener, 2001). These practices have an important signalling effect (Wayne et al., 2002) to employees given that they convey messages to them about organizational objectives and employees receive these messages, responding accordingly (Bowen and Ostroff, 2004; Den Hartog et al., 2004). By investing in HR practices such as training and performance appraisals, the organization can express its commitment to its employees in the long term and can show appreciation of their contributions with due consideration to their personal development and needs (Shuck et al., 2014; Yun et al., 2007). Thus, if implemented effectively, HPWS are likely to result in employees viewing themselves in a relationship characterized by mutual trust and support (Evans and Davis, 2005; Kehoe and Wright, 2013).

In applying social exchange theory to HPWS studies, HPWS practices can be seen as 'signals' which are interpreted by employees (Van De Voorde and Beijer, 2015). The perspective of social exchange relationships suggests that with exposure to similar HPWS practices within an organization, employees tend to develop a shared understanding of the exchange relationship with their manager (Chun et al., 2013). However, variations of exposure to HPWS practices exist among employee groups. Within the same employee group, employees develop different understandings of HPWS due to differences in factors, such as gender, values and preferences (Rousseau and Greller, 1994). These 'signals', therefore, can be understood idiosyncratically (Bowen and Ostroff, 2004).

A long-standing tradition of variance exists in HPWS, such as compensation, training and promotion opportunities among employees (Huselid, 1995). It has been found that management implements different HPWS practices in order to match different requirements of employee groups. Companies also use different HR practices to match the requirements of particular employee groups (Miles and Snow, 2007). For example, Lepak and Snell (2002) showed that core employees received significantly greater exposure to a work system that conveyed a high level of investment from employers, while non-core employee groups tended to be managed by lower levels of investment. In addition, Melian-Gonzalez and Verano-Tacoronte (2006) found that the work systems used for core employees were more sophisticated than those used for other employee groups. Lepak et al. (2007) also demonstrated that organizations tend to provide more participative opportunities for core employees than for other employees. Due to dissimilar HR practices across employees, a different employment status leads to differences in employees' exposure to HPWS practices. Such a difference is expected to contribute to employees' experiences and consequently the variability in employee perceptions of HPWS.

Moreover, if employees within the same employee group are subjected to the same set of HPWS, it does not necessarily mean their experiences are the same. This is another source of variability in employee perceptions of HPWS. For instance, the literature reveals differences between women and men who are similarly qualified and work in the same job within the same organization, suggesting the existence of differential treatment in management practices (Joshi et al., 2006). Likewise, employees tend to be weighted differently in the allocation of resources, such as pay and promotion; the procedures being used to allocate the resources; and the interpersonal treatment and information being shared with employees (Colquitt et al., 2001). Dissimilar resource allocation also causes disparities in employee experiences with HPWS practices. With regard to relational exchange, Graen and Uhl-Bien (1995) proposed that supervisors' social exchange relationships differed between subordinates. Employees who are close to their supervisor have the advantage of ample resources, more training opportunities, premier assignments, emotional support, decision-making responsibilities and cooperative interactions with the supervisor (Liden and Graen, 1980). Therefore, it is expected that such factors causing differences in employees' experiences with HPWS (such as gender and personal relationships with their supervisors) can be complex.

Manager interpretations of HPWS practices also provide the context within which employee perceptions of HPWS practices are formed (Liao et al., 2009). If employees perceive reality differently, then it is likely that not all employees interpret HPWS similarly (Nishii et al., 2008). A misalignment or disconnect could exist between manager and employee, and that could affect performance outcomes (Liao et al., 2009; Nishii et al., 2008). HR practices are most likely to lead to desired outcomes when employees perceive them consistently with managers' interpretations (Bowen and Ostroff, 2004).

In a relational exchange, managers' favourable attitudes, support and intentions have a positive effect on employees. Employees perceive management's intentions and attitudes through their interpretation of the way managers implement HR practices. Employee interpretation of HR practices varies in keeping with their experiences of these practices, and in accordance with a number of factors, such as difference in employment status, preference and relationship with their supervisors. Lepak et al. (2006) claim that previous research has primarily focused on managerial reports on the use of HPWS, ignoring the role of individual employees' actual experiences with these systems (Boon et al., 2011). Wright and Nishii (2012) noted that employees were affected by the extent to which they felt the HR practices implemented by the organization were indeed offered to them. Given the imbalanced research concentration, there have been calls for more research taking individual employee experiences and perceptions into consideration (Kehoe and Wright, 2013). Moreover, employees do not necessarily share the same interpretation as that of managers, whose interpretations of HPWS could provide a context for employees to form their own views and perceptions. The present research, therefore, examines employees' perceptions and their actual experiences of HPWS, taking into account the effect of managers' actions.

Trust

Trust is a positive relational construct in social exchange relationships (Dirks and Ferrin, 2002). It is identified as one of the critical determinants of individual and organizational effectiveness (Searle et al., 2011). Numerous studies have demonstrated the importance of trust in fostering positive outcomes for individuals and their organization (Agarwal, 2014; Dirks and Ferrin, 2001; Kong et al., 2014). Trust has been studied in literature at two levels: one is at a macro level, where employees build trust in their organization, while the other one is at a micro level, where employees build trust in individuals such as supervisors.

Trust in the organization

Employee perceptions of trust in the organization depend on the collective characteristics of the organization. This impression is lasting and is characterized by predictability, fairness, trustworthiness and good intentions (Ugwu et al., 2014).

Employee trust at the organizational level is claimed to be pivotal in explaining the effect of HPWS on employee performance and satisfaction in the workplace. In this stream of study, it is claimed that HPWS is a reflection of the organization's strategy (Gillespie and Dietz, 2009). HPWS create a social context in an organization, which informs employees about the intent and meaning of others' actions, thus affecting employees' attitudes and behaviours. For example, employee satisfaction with HR practices was associated with employee trust and commitment to the organization (Kinnie et al., 2005). The ways in which employees are managed and affected by HR practices also have a strong empirical relationship with trust and organizational performance (Wright and Haggerty, 2005)

Trust in supervisors

Although the implementation of HPWS reflects an organizational strategy, employees' supervisors are the representatives who send signals to employees about the value being placed on them by the organization. Supervisors interact with their subordinates and implement HR practices in conjunction with these subordinates; hence, both parties are believed to play a significant role in the causal chain of HPWS and outcomes (Den Hartog et al., 2004; Mathews and Illes, 2015; Snape and Redman, 2010). The role of supervisors is significant in the HPWS–performance chain and is widely acknowledged (Aryee et al., 2002; Boxall and Macky, 2014). Evidence illustrates that supervisors' roles in management extend beyond their traditional supervisory duties (Hales, 2005). They transmit the intent and meaning of top management policies and reflect the informal culture of the firm (Truss, 2001). Implementation of HPWS policies and practices relies on the action and support of employees' supervisors. In this sense, the quality of the relationship between employees and their immediate supervisors is liable to affect their perceptions of HPWS practices, either positively or negatively (Purcell and Hutchinson, 2007). Employee satisfaction and motivation are enhanced as attention from their supervisors increases (Purcell, 2003). The high quality of the employee–supervisor relationship has an impact on employees and then on the effective implementation of HPWS in the organization. Therefore, if employees perceive their supervisors to be trustworthy and supportive, their job satisfaction is likely to increase.

Trust and social exchange theory

Reciprocity emphasizes contingent bidirectional transactions, whereby something has to be given and something returned. For this reason, it involves mutual and complementary arrangements (Molm, 1994). In understanding workplace behaviours, the norm of reciprocity in social exchange theory (Blau, 1964) explains relationship building in the workplace. An action by one party leads to a response by another. With regard to HPWS studies, it is noted that employees form perceptions about intentions from the HPWS enacted by managers on the basis of the treatment they have received (Levinson, 1965). Employees see themselves as building a relationship with their supervisors.

Trust has been studied widely in the social exchange literature (Fox, 1974). It is an essential element of positive exchange relationships between people (Gould-Williams and Davies, 2005). Blau (1964) highlighted the role of trust in maintaining the social exchange relationship (Konovsky and Pugh, 1994). The presence of such a trust-based relationship has been found to stimulate employees' work engagement (Chughtai and Buckley, 2011), reduce emotional exhaustion (Lambert et al., 2012), lead to positive attitudes and behaviours (Burke et al., 2007), intensify knowledge and ideas exchange (Renzl, 2008; Wu et al., 2014), enhance performance (Neves and Caetano, 2009) and retain employees (Ertürk and Vurgun, 2015).

A social exchange relationship can be characterized by two types of trust. The first is affect-based trust (Chen et al., 1998). This trust reflects an emotional investment made by the individuals involved in which genuine care and concern are expressed, with a belief that these sentiments are reciprocated (McAllister, 1995). In this sense, the emotional ties linking individuals can provide the basis for trust. An individual's trustworthiness suggests an additive influence on the relational exchange (Butler, 1991). The other type of trust in a social exchange relationship is character-based trust (Zucker, 1986), which focuses on individuals' perceptions of another's character during the social exchange process. Drawing from this idea, Mayer et al. (1995) explained that perceptions of trustworthiness lead to trust. They further proposed that trustworthiness comprises ability, benevolence and integrity. Within the context of HPWS studies, supervisors' abilities are perceived by their subordinates according to the extent to which they have skills and competencies in their professional areas. Benevolence refers to employee perceptions of their supervisors in terms of how much they care about their subordinates. Integrity is the perception that their supervisors adhere to a set of acceptable principles. For example, managers have the authority to make decisions that have a significant impact on the employees (e.g., promotions, pay and work assignments). With trust, employees tend to believe that their supervisors are capable of making decisions in the best interest of employees and that the decisions are fair and justified.

In summary, this research adopts the theoretical framework of social exchange to illustrate the mediating role of trust. Trust is conceptualized as a critical factor in the social exchange process between employees and their immediate supervisors (Cafferkey and Dundon, 2015; Dirks and Ferrin, 2002). The two types of trust are simultaneously considered. The reasons for including two types of trust are, first, that social exchange involves the exchange of socio-emotional resources (Shore et al., 2006) and constitutes a broad investment in relationships, resulting in trust between employees and their supervisors. Second, employees form trust through their perceptions of their supervisors' characters (i.e., trustworthiness). Therefore, these two types of trust are indispensable components in understanding relational exchanges between employees and their supervisors at work.

Trust and HPWS

HPWS studies have not been limited to identifying whether HPWS practices lead to superior performance outcomes. They have also extended to understanding how HPWS practices influence employee job satisfaction and commitment. Trust is suggested as a variable explaining this process (Guest and Conway, 1999). Trust can be enhanced through a number of HPWS practices (Legge, 1995). These trust-inducing practices typically improve communication flow, foster empowerment and participation and encourage employees to invest both tangibly and emotionally in their organization (Ng et al., 2006). These practices shape employee behaviour and attitudes by aligning organizational goals with employees' goals (Arthur, 1994). When organizations fail to deliver a promise, however, employees' faith and trust diminish (Macneil, 1985). Employee perceptions of what is owed and what they are prepared to offer to the organization are negatively affected, and work performance could also be jeopardized (Robinson et al., 1994).

Although there is no consensus as to which HR practices should be included in HPWS, an important feature of HPWS is employee participation that enhances performance. In particular, participation that includes frequent and open communication enhances levels of trust within an organization (Sydow, 1998). Frequent communication between managers and employees encourages mutual trust to grow (Cohen-Charash and Spector, 2001). Additionally, there are a number of other HR practices that encourage the development of trust relationships. Job security, as one component of HPWS, is argued to enhance trust in the workplace as well (Carnevale and Wechsler, 1992). In terms of performance appraisal systems, Mayer and Davis (1999) argued that management's ability to manage the workforce and managers' willingness to recognize and reward employees' contributions enhance trust in management. In addition, training is seen by employees as an investment by the organization and consequently signals an organization's concern for its employees' interests. Hence, training can be associated with trust (Tannenbaum and Davis, 1969).

With increased attention to employee outcomes, trust is also linked to a number of attitudinal outcomes such as job satisfaction. Rich (1997) suggested that perceived high levels of trustworthiness of managers made employees feel safe and positive about their managers. Specifically, managers are responsible for many duties that significantly affect employees' job satisfaction, such as performance appraisals, training and promotion. Employees are likely to feel comfortable when they trust their managers. Having a low level of trust in a manager is likely to be psychologically distressing especially when the manager has power over important aspects of an employee's job and work life, and this distress is likely to affect employee job satisfaction in the workplace. An association between trust and overall satisfaction has also been found (Ellis and Shockley-Zalabak, 2001; Kim, 2002; Morley et al., 2007; Yang and Kassekert, 2010). Moreover, trust is found to generate job satisfaction by meeting employees' needs at work, such as the need for communication (Ellis and Shockley-Zalabak, 2001; Fried, 1991; Rayton and Yalabik, 2014), and employees' feelings of being protected by their supervisors/managers (Carnevale and Wechsler, 1992).

In addition, studies have shown that a salient outcome of trust is a diminished intention to leave by employees (Tan and Tan, 2000). Based on the norm of reciprocity, when employees perceive themselves as being valued and cared for by their supervisors, they respond with high levels of trust. This employee perception is likely to lead to employees' attachment to their employers (Spreitzer and Mishra, 2002) while lowering their intention to leave – a link which is supported by research (Konovsky and Cropanzano, 1991; Mishra and Morrissey, 1990; Wong et al., 2015).

In this research, trust is proposed to be an important intervening variable in the relationship between HPWS and employee outcomes. Within the framework of the social exchange theory, relationships between people evolve over time into trust, loyalty and mutual commitment (Cropanzano and Mitchell, 2005). With the implementation of HPWS, employees interpret organizational actions such as HPWS practices and the trustworthiness of management as indicative of how they are valued and respected (Whitener, 2001). When employees perceive that their managers are trustworthy, they are likely to take risks, do extra work (Oketch, 2004) and feel attached to their employers (Spreitzer and Mishra,

2002), which possibly lowers the turnover rate. Moreover, employees believe that they are valued, which fosters feelings of trustworthiness towards management (Spreitzer and Mishra, 2002) and is likely to increase job satisfaction and possible overall performance.

HPWS and individual performance

SHRM studies have extensively tested the HPWS–performance relationship. A number of studies report a positive association between HPWS practices and organizational performance. Understanding this relationship is one of the essential pursuits of HPWS research (Becker et al., 1998). For example, studies conducted by Combs et al. (2006) and Wright et al. (2005) suggested a link between HPWS and organizational market outcomes at the organizational level. A link is also established between HPWS and financial outcomes (Choi, 2014; Messersmith and Guthrie, 2010).

This growing interest is easy to understand because HPWS are mainly perceived and implemented from managerial perspectives. Managers seek to achieve superior organizational outcomes through HR practices rather than employee outcomes such as job satisfaction. A critical perspective is developed which suggests a stronger focus on an employee-oriented perspective. Employees are important in HPWS studies because HR practices are likely to have the most immediate impact on employees since they are in a closer line of sight to these practices (Dyer and Reeves, 1995). Given the importance of employees and the lack of studies on this subject, there has been a call for studies to place in central position the effects of HPWS on employees (Delbridge and Keenoy, 2010; Paauwe, 2009).

The limited empirical research on the impact of HPWS on employee outcomes reports mixed or even contradictory findings (Ramsay et al., 2000). For example, Macky and Boxall (2008) found that greater experience of HPWS can lead to either higher job satisfaction or dissatisfaction depending on workload and working hours. Wood and De Menezes (2011) found that HPWS increase employee anxiety and are not related to job satisfaction. Godard (2001) found that some HPWS practices such as job rotation and multi-skilling have no significant relationship to job satisfaction and that, in fact, some practices, such as team autonomy, have a negative relationship to job satisfaction. García-Chas et al. (2016) found that HPWS exerted a stronger effect on job satisfaction among employees with low motivation than those with high motivation. Van De Voorde and Beijer (2015) associated HPWS with employee outcomes. They showed that HR well-being attributions were associated with a higher level of employee commitment and a lower level of job strain. They also demonstrated that HR performance attributions were associated with higher levels of job strain. The mixed findings regarding the relationship between HPWS and employee well-being suggest that the effects of HR practices on employee well-being are complex. It is questioned whether the statistical models used to examine the relationship between HPWS and employee well-being are too simplistic to capture the complex reality of implementation and operation of HPWS (Ramsay et al., 2000).

Research framework and hypotheses

The notion of HPWS has sparked widespread interest in the past decades. It is described as a set of systems designed to ensure that the HR practices adopted lead in some way to superior organizational performance (Boxall and Macky, 2009). In HPWS, the bundling of practices is critical. Practices are combined into a bundle which shapes the pattern of interactions between managers and employees (MacDuffie, 1995).

As mentioned earlier, the HR system (HPWS) can affect performance on multiple levels (Boxall and Macky, 2009). One level is individual employees' ability, motivation and opportunities to perform (Huselid, 1995). The HR system in this case works through its impacts on the skills and knowledge of employees, their willingness to exert effort and their opportunities to utilize their skills at work. The HR system can also exert influence on a more collective level, such as influencing social climate and dealing with employee voice (Wood and Wall, 2007). The individual and collective levels are inextricably linked. Individuals' abilities, opportunities to perform and motivations are influenced by the quality of resources, collaboration and trust in their working environment. The HR system discussed in this book, namely HPWS, helps enhance trust in management to improve the quality of relationships between groups (Leana and Van Buren, 1999). The dimensions of HPWS applied in this research include staffing, training, job descriptions, internal mobility, performance appraisals, job security, rewarding, and employee participation. The choice of these dimensions is based on studies by Bamberger and Meshoulam (2000); it covers several frequently identified and tested domains in HPWS literature.

In HPWS literature, a key premise is that HPWS depend on positive responses from employees (Godard, 2004; Macky and Boxall, 2007). Workplace (organizational) performance is influenced by team performance, which is preceded by individual job performance. Therefore, it is suggested that assessments of the effects of HPWS depend on obtaining relevant data on employee outcomes (Appelbaum, 2000). Employee interpretations of intended and implemented HPWS impact their attitudes and behaviour at work (Nishii et al., 2008), followed by their individual job performance. Individual employees form different interpretations and understandings of implemented HPWS. Employees also interpret HPWS differently from managers. This inconsistency is likely to be caused by variability in implementation and diverse individual-level cognitive schemes (Edgar and Geare, 2005; Khilji and Wang, 2006; Wright and Haggerty, 2005). In addition, the majority of HPWS studies are investigated from a managerial perspective in a top-down approach. Studies on employee perceptions remain sparse. This research aims to fill the gap by taking a bottom-up approach and by considering employees' perceptions of HPWS and the effects on employee outcomes.

Moreover, HPWS studies are not limited to understanding what constitutes HPWS and the relationship between organizational and individual outcomes. This book extends its scope to explore how the HPWS themselves work. In an attempt to explore the mediating factor, social exchange theory (Blau, 1964) is chosen to provide the explanatory framework. In the work of Eisenberger et al. (1990), it is claimed that trust is essential to social exchange relations because social exchange requires trusting others to discharge obligation and to reciprocate. With a mutual trust relationship at work, managers and employees tend to work together efficiently, which possibly leads to the effective realization of HPWS (Seabright et al., 1992).

The conceptual research model is presented in Figure 2.1, combining components discussed prior, such as employees' perceptions, trust and employee outcomes. It suggests an association between employee perceptions of HPWS and employees' job satisfaction and their intention to stay with their current employer. Employee perception on management's trustworthiness is proposed as a mediator in the relationship between perceived HPWS, job satisfaction and turnover intention respectively. A more detailed analysis will be presented in chapter 5.

In HPWS literature, job satisfaction plays a vital role for employees. Studies have established and tested the positive relationship between HPWS and job satisfaction. For example, Appelbaum (2000) found that HPWS led to increased trust in management, followed by job satisfaction, in the case of steel and medical electronics workers. Vandenberg et al. (1999) associated HR practices with improved employee job satisfaction. In addition, studies found that job satisfaction was influenced by certain HR dimensions, such as opportunities to participate (Guest et al., 2003), job security (Yousef, 1998) and training opportunities (Guzzo and Noonan, 1994). HPWS is proved to impact job satisfaction positively, mostly in the West; however, relevant studies in the context of China are limited. The positive relationship between HPWS and job satisfaction is expected to extend to SOEs and DPEs in China; therefore, the first hypothesis of the present study is:

> *Hypothesis 1: Employees' perception of adopted HPWS is positively related to employee job satisfaction.*

Empirical studies have shown that the implementation of HPWS is negatively related to intentions to leave and employee turnover rate (as an indicator

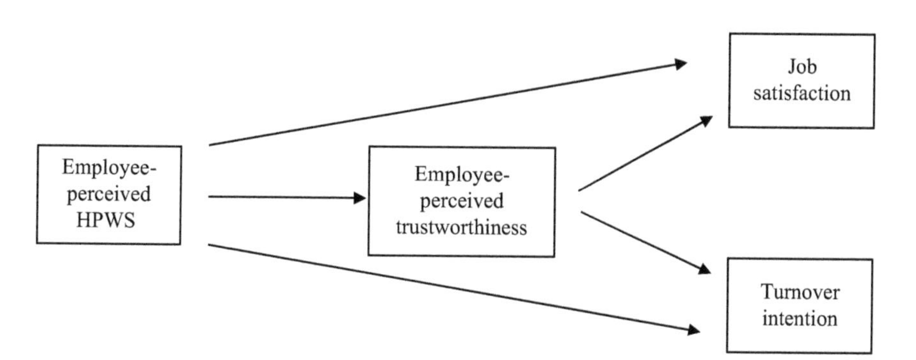

Figure 2.1 Conceptual research model

of organizational performance). Studies have typically been conducted at the organizational level and often rely on measurements at that level (Guthrie, 2001; Huselid, 1995; Shaw et al., 2009; Way, 2002). These studies have mostly used data from the West. Studies on these issues in the East remain sparse. In addition, research on employee turnover has not adequately considered individuals' attitudes that drive their intention to leave. Therefore, this book proposes to assess the relationship at the individual level. It is expected that a negative relationship exists in Chinese SOEs and DPEs between employee perceptions and their intention to leave. Hence, we define the second hypothesis as:

Hypothesis 2: Employees' perception of adopted HPWS is negatively related to employees' intention to leave.

Blau's (1964) formulation of the social exchange relationship highlighted the role of trust. A social exchange–based relationship in the workplace can be characterized by character-based trust and affect-based trust (McAllister, 1995). Employee trust in managers is centred on how managers make decisions that affect employees and how managers behave (Luhmann and Schorr, 1979). In the workplace, managers make decisions on issues which affect employees, such as promotion, allocation of benefits and training. In terms of character-based trust, employees form perceptions on whether managers are capable of and reliable in making these decisions. The formation of employee perceptions is possibly based on the decisions made in the past. In other words, employees' assessment of what and how HR policies and practices have been adopted impact their perceptions of managers' trustworthiness. If the HR policies and practices are perceived to be effective, employees tend to perceive their managers as being capable and reliable, consequently leading to a high level of trust. In terms of affect-based trust, HPWS may be viewed by employees as an intention of long-term investment in them. Implementation of HPWS signals to employees that they are valued and cared for by managers. Employees may thus develop high trust in their supervisors/managers. Moreover, managerial work involves complexity, uncertainty and mutual considerations. Under conditions of uncertainty and complexity, sustained effective communication is required (Thompson, 1967). The implementation of HPWS encourages employee participation in managerial decision-making, which facilitates sustained effective communication. In this sense, employees tend to feel that their opinions are being taken into consideration and then possibly form trust in managers.

According to social exchange theory, favourable or spontaneous gestures of good-will by managers in an employment relationship engender an obligation on the part of employees to reciprocate the good deeds of the managers. Social exchange requires trusting others to reciprocate. By adopting and implementing HPWS, managers intend to demonstrate that they are capable and reliable at work, that they behave in the interests of employees and that they value employees and their contributions. If employees perceive and interpret the implementation of HPWS as managers expect, they may form a high level of trust towards managers. With high levels of trust, employees tend to reciprocate with discretionary behaviours (e.g., low turnover intention) and positive attitudes (e.g., job satisfaction). This reciprocity by employees is supported by studies (Gong et al., 2010; Shaw et al., 2009) which indicate that in the presence of trust, employees feel obligated to behave discretionally and make contributions to employers.

In HPWS literature, the relationship between trust and employee attitudes and behaviours is supported. For example, employees are motivated when they feel that they are cared for in the employment relationship, and hence they demonstrate positive attitudes and behaviours (Rich et al., 2010; Saks, 2006). Other studies (Cropanzano et al., 2003; Kuvaas and Dysvik, 2010) have presented similar conclusions in terms of employees demonstrating positive attitudes and behaviours when their contributions are recognized. Konovsky and Pugh (1994) stated that there was a paucity of research in the examination of the role of trust in explicating employee outcomes. As discussed earlier, trust is suggested as a way to mediate the relationship between employee perceptions on the implementation of HPWS and job satisfaction and turnover intention. Therefore, we define the last three hypotheses as:

Hypothesis 3: Employees' perception of adopted HPWS is positively related to employees' trust of management.

Hypothesis 4: Employees' trust of management mediates the positive relationships between HPWS and job satisfaction.

Hypothesis 5: Employees' trust of management mediates the negative relationships between HPWS and employees' intention to leave.

Conclusion

This chapter reviews transition from HRM to SHRM, HPWS, social exchange theory and trust. Among these studies, SHRM/HPWS is mainly understood as a West-oriented concept. Since China is embracing global challenges and opportunities, this ideology is also adopted and applied by Chinese enterprises. Unlike their Western counterparts, the implementation of SHRM/HPWS in China shows its own characteristics. The next chapter will elaborate on details of SHRM/HPWS studies in China.

References

Agarwal, U. A. 2014. Linking justice, trust and innovative work behaviour to work engagement. *Personnel Review*, 43, 41–73.

Allen, D. G., Shore, L. M. and Griffeth, R. W. 2003. The role of perceived organizational support and supportive human resource practices in the turnover process. *Journal of Management*, 29, 99–118.

Ambrose, M. L. and Schminke, M. 2003. Organization structure as a moderator of the relationship between procedural justice, interactional justice, perceived organizational support, and supervisory trust. *Journal of Applied Psychology*, 88, 295.

Appelbaum, E. 2000. *Manufacturing advantage: Why high-performance work systems pay off*, Ithaca, NY: Cornell University Press.

Armstrong, C., Flood, P. C., Guthrie, J. P., Liu, W., Maccurtain, S. and Mkamwa, T. 2010. The impact of diversity and equality management on firm performance: Beyond high performance work systems. *Human Resource Management*, 49, 977–998.

Arthur, J. B. 1994. Effects of human resource systems on manufacturing performance and turnover. *Academy of Management Journal*, 37, 670–687.

Aryee, S., Budhwar, P. S. and Chen, Z. X. 2002. Trust as a mediator of the relationship between organizational justice and work outcomes: Test of a social exchange model. *Journal of Organizational Behavior*, 23, 267–285.

Aselage, J. and Eisenberger, R. 2003. Perceived organizational support and psychological contracts: A theoretical integration. *Journal of Organizational Behavior*, 24, 491–509.

Bae, J. and Lawler, J. J. 2000. Organizational and HRM strategies in Korea: Impact on firm performance in an emerging economy. *Academy of Management Journal*, 43, 502–517.

Bamberger, P. and Meshoulam, I. 2000. *Human resource management strategy*, London: Published Sage.

Barney, J. 1991. Firm resources and sustained competitive advantage. *Journal of Management*, 17, 99–120.

Barraud-Didier, V., Henninger, M.-C. and El Akremi, A. 2012. The relationship between members' trust and participation in the governance of cooperatives: The role of organizational commitment. *International Food and Agribusiness Management Review*, 15, 1–24.

Bartram, T., Stanton, P., Leggat, S., Casimir, G. and Fraser, B. 2007. Lost in translation: Exploring the link between HRM and performance in healthcare. *Human Resource Management Journal*, 17, 21–41.

Batt, R. 2002. Managing customer services: Human resource practices, quit rates, and sales growth. *Academy of Management Journal*, 45, 587–597.

Becker, B. E. and Gerhart, B. 1996. The impact of human resource management on organizational performance: Progress and prospects. *Academy of Management Journal*, 39, 779–801.

Becker, B. and Huselid, M. A. 1998. High performance work systems and firm performance: A synthesis of research and managerial implications. *Research in Personnel and Human Resource Management*, 16, 53–101.

Becker, B. E., Huselid, M. A., Pickus, P. S. and Spratt, M. F. 1997. HR as a source of shareholder value: Research and recommendations. *Human Resource Management*, 36, 39–47.

Bhatnagar, J. 2007. Predictors of organizational commitment in India: Strategic HR roles, organizational learning capability and psychological empowerment. *The International Journal of Human Resource Management*, 18, 1782–1811.

Blau, P. M. 1964. *Exchange and power in social life*, Piscataway, NJ: Transaction Publishers.

Boon, C., Belschak, F. D., Den Hartog, D. N. and Pijnenburg, M. 2014. Perceived human resource management practices. *Journal of Personnel Psychology*, 13(1), 21–33.

Boon, C., Den Hartog, D. N., Boselie, P. and Paauwe, J. 2011. The relationship between perceptions of HR practices and employee outcomes: Examining the role of person–organisation and person–job fit. *The International Journal of Human Resource Management*, 22, 138–162.

Bowen, D. E. and Lawler, E. E. 1992. Total quality-oriented human resources management. *Organizational Dynamics*, 20, 29–41.

Bowen, D. E. and Ostroff, C. 2004. Understanding HRM–firm performance linkages: The role of the 'strength' of the HRM system. *Academy of Management Review*, 29, 203–221.

Boxall, P. and Macky, K. 2009. Research and theory on high-performance work systems: Progressing the high-involvement stream. *Human Resource Management Journal*, 19, 3–23.

Boxall, P. and Macky, K. 2014. High-involvement work processes, work intensification and employee well-being. *Work, Employment & Society*, 28, 963–984.

Burke, C. S., Sims, D. E., Lazzara, E. H. and Salas, E. 2007. Trust in leadership: A multi-level review and integration. *The Leadership Quarterly*, 18, 606–632.

Burris, E. R., Detert, J. R. and Romney, A. C. 2013. Speaking up vs. being heard: The disagreement around and outcomes of employee voice. *Organization Science*, 24, 22–38.

Burt, C. D. 1992. Retrieval characteristics of autobiographical memories: Event and date information. *Applied Cognitive Psychology*, 6, 389–404.

Butler, J. K. 1991. Toward understanding and measuring conditions of trust: Evolution of a conditions of trust inventory. *Journal of Management*, 17, 643–663.

Cafferkey, K. and Dundon, T. 2015. Explaining the black box: HPWS and organisational climate. *Personnel Review*, 44, 666–688.

Carnevale, D. G. and Wechsler, B. 1992. Trust in the public sector individual and organizational determinants. *Administration & Society*, 23, 471–494.

Chen, C. C., Chen, X.-P. and Meindl, J. R. 1998. How can cooperation be fostered? The cultural effects of individualism-collectivism. *Academy of Management Review*, 23, 285–304.

Choi, J.-H. 2014. Who should be the respondent? Comparing predictive powers between managers' and employees' responses in measuring high-performance work systems practices. *The International Journal of Human Resource Management*, 25, 2667–2680.

Chughtai, A. A. and Buckley, F. 2011. Work engagement: Antecedents, the mediating role of learning goal orientation and job performance. *Career Development International*, 16, 684–705.

Chun, J. S., Shin, Y., Choi, J. N. and Kim, M. S. 2013. How does corporate ethics contribute to firm financial performance? The mediating role of collective organizational commitment and organizational citizenship behavior. *Journal of Management*, 39, 853–877.

Cohen-Charash, Y. and Spector, P. E. 2001. The role of justice in organizations: A meta-analysis. *Organizational Behavior and Human Decision Processes*, 86, 278–321.

Colquitt, J. A., Conlon, D. E., Wesson, M. J., Porter, C. O. and Ng, K. Y. 2001. Justice at the millennium: A meta-analytic review of 25 years of organizational justice research. *Journal of Applied Psychology*, 86, 425–445.

Combs, J., Liu, Y., Hall, A. and Ketchen, D. 2006. How much do high-performance work practices matter? A meta-analysis of their effects on organizational performance. *Personnel Psychology*, 59, 501–528.

Cropanzano, R. and Mitchell, M. S. 2005. Social exchange theory: An interdisciplinary review. *Journal of Management*, 31, 874–900.

Cropanzano, R., Rupp, D. E. and Byrne, Z. S. 2003. The relationship of emotional exhaustion to work attitudes, job performance, and organizational citizenship behaviors. *Journal of Applied Psychology*, 88, 160–169.

Datta, D. K., Guthrie, J. P. and Wright, P. M. 2005. Human resource management and labor productivity: Does industry matter? *Academy of Management Journal*, 48, 135–145.

Davies, M.-A., Laschinger, H. K. S. and Andrusyszyn, M.-A. 2006. Clinical educators' empowerment, job tension, and job satisfaction: A test of Kanter's theory. *Journal for Nurses in Professional Development*, 22, 78–86.

Deconinck, J. B. 2010. The effect of organizational justice, perceived organizational support, and perceived supervisor support on marketing employees' level of trust. *Journal of Business Research*, 63, 1349–1355.

Delbridge, R. and Keenoy, T. 2010. Beyond managerialism? *The International Journal of Human Resource Management*, 21, 799–817.

Delery, J. E. 1998. Issues of fit in strategic human resource management: Implications for research. *Human Resource Management Review*, 8, 289–309.

Delery, J. E. and Doty, D. H. 1996. Modes of theorizing in strategic human resource management: Tests of universalistic, contingency, and configurational performance predictions. *Academy of Management Journal*, 39, 802–835.

Delery, J. E. and Shaw, J. D. 2001. The strategic management of people in work organizations: Review, synthesis, and extension. In: Ferris, G. R. (ed.) *Research in Personnel and Human Resources Management*. Stanford, CT: JAI Press

Den Hartog, D. N., Boon, C., Verburg, R. M. and Croon, M. A. 2013. HRM, communication, satisfaction, and perceived performance a cross-level test. *Journal of Management*, 39, 1637–1665.

Den Hartog, D. N., Boselie, P. and Paauwe, J. 2004. Performance management: A model and research agenda. *Applied Psychology*, 53, 556–569.

Dirks, K. T. and Ferrin, D. L. 2001. The role of trust in organizational settings. *Organization Science*, 12, 450–467.

Dirks, K. T. and Ferrin, D. L. 2002. Trust in leadership: Meta-analytic findings and implications for research and practice. *Journal of Applied Psychology*, 87, 611.

Druker, J., White, G., Hegewisch, A. and Mayne, L. 1996. Between hard and soft HRM: Human resource management in the construction industry. *Construction Management & Economics*, 14, 405–416.

Dyer, L. and Reeves, T. 1995. Human resource strategies and firm performance: What do we know and where do we need to go? *International Journal of Human Resource Management*, 6, 656–670.

Edgar, F. and Geare, A. 2005. HRM practice and employee attitudes: Different measures-different results. *Personnel Review*, 34, 534–549.

Eisenberger, R., Armeli, S., Rexwinkel, B., Lynch, P. D. and Rhoades, L. 2001. Reciprocation of perceived organizational support. *Journal of Applied Psychology*, 86, 42.

Eisenberger, R., Fasolo, P. and Davis-Lamastro, V. 1990. Perceived organizational support and employee diligence, commitment, and innovation. *Journal of Applied Psychology*, 75, 51.

Eisenberger, R., Shoss, M. K., Karagonlar, G., Gonzalez-Morales, M. G., Wickham, R. E. and Buffardi, L. C. 2014. The supervisor POS–LMX–subordinate POS chain: Moderation by reciprocation wariness and supervisor's organizational embodiment. *Journal of Organizational Behavior*, 35, 635–656.

Ellis, K. and Shockley-Zalabak, P. 2001. Trust in top management and immediate supervisor: The relationship to satisfaction, perceived organizational effectiveness, and information receiving. *Communication Quarterly*, 49, 382–398.

Elloy, D. 2012. Effects of ability utilization, job influence and organization commitment on employee empowerment: An empirical study. *International Journal of Management*, 29, 627.

Elorza, U., Harris, C., Aritzeta, A., Balluerka, N., Garavan, T. and Pezet, E. 2016. The effect of management and employee perspectives of high-performance work systems on employees' discretionary behaviour. *Personnel Review*, 45, 121–141.

Emerson, R. M. 1976. Social exchange theory. In: Rosenberg, M. and Turner, R. H. (eds.) *Social Psychology: Sociological Perspectives*. New York: Basic Books.

Ensher, E. A., Thomas, C. and Murphy, S. E. 2001. Comparison of traditional, step-ahead, and peer mentoring on protégés' support, satisfaction, and perceptions of career success: A social exchange perspective. *Journal of Business and Psychology*, 15, 419–438.

Ertürk, A. and Vurgun, L. 2015. Retention of IT professionals: Examining the influence of empowerment, social exchange, and trust. *Journal of Business Research*, 68, 34–46.

Evans, W. R. and Davis, W. D. 2005. High-performance work systems and organizational performance: The mediating role of internal social structure. *Journal of Management*, 31, 758–775.

Farmer, S. M., Van Dyne, L. and Kamdar, D. 2015. The contextualized self: How team–member exchange leads to coworker identification and helping OCB. *Journal of Applied Psychology*, 100, 583.

Fernandez, S. and Moldogaziev, T. A. 2011. causal model of the empowerment process: Exploring the links between empowerment practices, employee cognitions, and behavioral outcomes. Prepared for the National Public Management Research Conference.

Fernandez, S. and Moldogaziev, T. A. 2013. Employee empowerment, employee attitudes, and performance: Testing a causal model. *Public Administration Review*, 73, 490–506.

Flynn, F. J. 2003. How much should I give and how often? The effects of generosity and frequency of favor exchange on social status and productivity. *Academy of Management Journal*, 46, 539–553.

Fox, A. 1974. *Beyond contract: Work, power and trust relations*, London: Faber & Faber.

Fried, Y. 1991. Meta-analytic comparison of the Job Diagnostic Survey and Job Characteristics Inventory as correlates of work satisfaction and performance. *Journal of Applied Psychology*, 76, 690.

Fulford, M. D. and Enz, C. A. 1995. The impact of empowerment on service employees. *Journal of Managerial Issues*, 161–175.

Gao, L., Janssen, O. and Shi, K. 2011. Leader trust and employee voice: The moderating role of empowering leader behaviors. *The Leadership Quarterly*, 22, 787–798.

García-Chas, R., Neira-Fontela, E. and Varela-Neira, C. 2016. High-performance work systems and job satisfaction: A multilevel model. *Journal of Managerial Psychology*, 31, 451–466.

Gillespie, N. and Dietz, G. 2009. Trust repair after an organization-level failure. *Academy of Management Review*, 34, 127–145.

Godard, J. 2001. High performance and the transformation of work? The implications of alternative work practices for the experience and outcomes of work. *Industrial & Labor Relations Review*, 54, 776–805.

Godard, J. 2004. A critical assessment of the high-performance paradigm. *British Journal of Industrial Relations*, 42, 349–378.

Golden, T. D. and Veiga, J. F. 2015. Self-estrangement's toll on job performance the pivotal role of social exchange relationships with coworkers. *Journal of Management*, 261–271.

Gong, Y., Chang, S. and Cheung, S. Y. 2010. High performance work system and collective OCB: A collective social exchange perspective. *Human Resource Management Journal*, 20, 119–137.

Gordon, G., Gilley, A., Avery, S., Gilley, J. W. and Barber, A. 2014. Employee perceptions of the manager behaviors that create follower-leader trust. *Management and Organizational Studies*, 1, 44.

Gouldner, A. W. 1960. The norm of reciprocity: A preliminary statement. *American Sociological Review*, 25, 161–178.

Gould-Williams, J. 2003. The importance of HR practices and workplace trust in achieving superior performance: A study of public-sector organizations. *International Journal of Human Resource Management*, 14, 28–54.

Gould-Williams, J. and Davies, F. 2005. Using social exchange theory to predict the effects of HRM practice on employee outcomes: An analysis of public sector workers. *Public Management Review*, 7, 1–24.

Graen, G. B. and Scandura, T. A. 1987. Toward a psychology of dyadic organizing. In: Cummings, L.L. and Staw, B.M. (eds.) *Research in Organizational Behavior* (Vol. 9), 175–208. Greenwich, CT: JAI Press.

Graen, G. B. and Uhl-Bien, M. 1995. Relationship-based approach to leadership: Development of leader-member exchange (LMX) theory of leadership over 25 years: Applying a multi-level multi-domain perspective. *The Leadership Quarterly*, 6, 219–247.

Greenberg, J. 1990. Organizational justice: Yesterday, today, and tomorrow. *Journal of Management*, 16, 399–432.

Guest, D. E. 2001. Human resource management: When research confronts theory. *International Journal of Human Resource Management*, 12, 1092–1106.

Guest, D. E. 2002. Human resource management, corporate performance and employee wellbeing: Building the worker into HRM. *Journal of Industrial Relations*, 44, 335–358.

Guest, D. E. and Conway, N. 1999. Peering into the black hole: The downside of the new employment relations in the UK. *British Journal of Industrial Relations*, 37, 367–389.

Guest, D. E. and Grant, B. 1991. The complex action of phosphonates as antifungal agents. *Biological Reviews*, 66, 159–187.

Guest, D. E., Michie, J., Conway, N. and Sheehan, M. 2003. Human resource management and corporate performance in the UK. *British Journal of Industrial Relations*, 41, 291–314.

Guthrie, J. P. 2001. High-involvement work practices, turnover, and productivity: Evidence from New Zealand. *Academy of Management Journal*, 44, 180–190.

Guthrie, J. P., Flood, P. C., Liu, W. and Maccurtain, S. 2009. High performance work systems in Ireland: Human resource and organizational outcomes. *The International Journal of Human Resource Management*, 20, 112–125.

Guzzo, R. A. and Noonan, K. A. 1994. Human resource practices as communications and the psychological contract. *Human Resource Management*, 33, 447–462.

Hales, C. 2005. Rooted in supervision, branching into management: Continuity and change in the role of first-line manager. *Journal of Management Studies*, 42, 471–506.

Huselid, M. A. 1995. The impact of human resource management practices on turnover, productivity, and corporate financial performance. *Academy of Management Journal*, 38, 635–672.

Ichniowski, C. and Shaw, K. 1999. The effects of human resource management systems on economic performance: An international comparison of US and Japanese plants. *Management Science*, 45, 704–721.

Joshi, A., Liao, H. and Jackson, S. E. 2006. Cross-level effects of workplace diversity on sales performance and pay. *Academy of Management Journal*, 49, 459–481.

Kanter, R. M. and Stein, B. 1979. *Life in organizations: Workplaces as people experience them*, New York: Basic Books.

Kehoe, R. R. and Wright, P. M. 2013. The impact of high-performance human resource practices on employees' attitudes and behaviors. *Journal of Management*, 39, 366–391.

Khilji, S. E. and Wang, X. 2006. 'Intended' and 'implemented' HRM: The missing linchpin in strategic human resource management research. *The International Journal of Human Resource Management*, 17, 1171–1189.

Kim, B., Losekoot, E. and Milne, S. 2013. Consequences of empowerment among restaurant servers: Helping behaviors and average check size. *Management Decision*, 51, 781–794.

Kim, S. 2002. Participative management and job satisfaction: Lessons for management leadership. *Public Administration Review*, 62, 231–241.

Kinnie, N., Hutchinson, S., Purcell, J., Rayton, B. and Swart, J. 2005. Satisfaction with HR practices and commitment to the organisation: Why one size does not fit all. *Human Resource Management Journal*, 15, 9–29.

Knoll, M. and Redman, T. 2015. Does the presence of voice imply the absence of silence? The necessity to consider employees' affective attachment and job engagement. *Human Resource Management*, 55(5), 829–844.

Kochan, T. and Osterman, P. 1995. *Mutual gains*, Boston, MA: Harvard Business School.

Kong, D. T., Dirks, K. T. and Ferrin, D. L. 2014. Interpersonal trust within negotiations: Meta-analytic evidence, critical contingencies, and directions for future research. *Academy of Management Journal*, 57, 1235–1255.

Konovsky, M. A. and Cropanzano, R. 1991. Perceived fairness of employee drug testing as a predictor of employee attitudes and job performance. *Journal of Applied Psychology*, 76, 698.

Konovsky, M. A. and Pugh, S. D. 1994. Citizenship behavior and social exchange. *Academy of Management Journal*, 37, 656–669.

Krosgaard, M. A., Brodt, S. E. and Whitener, E. M. 2002. Trust in the face of conflict: The role of managerial trustworthy behavior and organizational context. *Journal of Applied Psychology*, 87, 312.

Kuvaas, B. 2008. An exploration of how the employee–organization relationship affects the linkage between perception of developmental human resource practices and employee outcomes*. *Journal of Management Studies*, 45, 1–25.

Kuvaas, B. and Dysvik, A. 2010. Exploring alternative relationships between perceived investment in employee development, perceived supervisor support and employee outcomes. *Human Resource Management Journal*, 20, 138–156.

Lambert, E. G., Hogan, N. L., Barton-Bellessa, S. M. and Jiang, S. 2012. Examining the relationship between supervisor and management trust and job burnout among correctional staff. *Criminal Justice and Behavior*, 39, 938–957.

Lawler, E. E. 1986. *High-involvement management*. San Francisco: Jossey-Bass..

Lawler, J. J., Chen, S.-J., Wu, P.-C., Bae, J. and Bai, B. 2011. High-performance work systems in foreign subsidiaries of American multinationals: An institutional model. *Journal of International Business Studies*, 42, 202–220.

Leana, C. R. and Van Buren, H. J. 1999. Organizational social capital and employment practices. *Academy of Management Review*, 24, 538–555.

Lee, H., Cayer, N. J. and Lan, G. Z. 2006. Changing federal government employee attitudes since the Civil Service Reform Act of 1978. *Review of Public Personnel Administration*, 26, 21–51.

Legge, K. 1995. HRM: Rhetoric, reality and hidden agendas. *Human Resource Management: A Critical Text*, London: Routledge, 33–59.

Legge, K. 2005. *Human resource management: Rhetorics and realities*, Anniversary Edition, Palgrave Macmillan.

Lepak, D. P., Liao, H., Chung, Y. and Harden, E. E. 2006. A conceptual review of human resource management systems in strategic human resource management research. *Research in Personnel and Human Resources Management*, 25, 217–271.

Lepak, D. P. and Snell, S. A. 2002. Examining the human resource architecture: The relationships among human capital, employment, and human resource configurations. *Journal of Management*, 28, 517–543.

Lepak, D. P., Taylor, M. S., Tekleab, A. G., Marrone, J. A. and Cohen, D. J. 2007. An examination of the use of high-investment human resource systems for core and support employees. *Human Resource Management*, 46, 223–246.

Levinson, H. 1965. Reciprocation: The relationship between man and organization. *Administrative Science Quarterly*, 9, 370–390.

Liao, H., Toya, K., Lepak, D. P. and Hong, Y. 2009. Do they see eye to eye? Management and employee perspectives of high-performance work systems and influence processes on service quality. *Journal of Applied Psychology*, 94, 371–391.

Liden, R. C. and Graen, G. 1980. Generalizability of the vertical dyad linkage model of leadership. *Academy of Management Journal*, 23, 451–465.

Liden, R. C., Sparrowe, R. T. and Wayne, S. J. 1997. Leader-member exchange theory: The past and potential for the future. *Research in Personnel and Human Resources Management*, 15, 47–120.

Liden, R. C., Wayne, S. J. and Sparrowe, R. T. 2000. An examination of the mediating role of psychological empowerment on the relations between the job, interpersonal relationships, and work outcomes. *Journal of Applied Psychology*, 85, 407–416.

Ling, Y. and Kellermanns, F. W. 2010. The effects of family firm specific sources of TMT diversity: The moderating role of information exchange frequency. *Journal of Management Studies*, 47, 322–344.

Luhmann, N. and Schorr, K. E. 1979. *Reflexionsprobleme im Erziehungssystem*, Stuttgart: Klett-Cotta.

Macduffie, J. P. 1995. Human resource bundles and manufacturing performance: Organizational logic and flexible production systems in the world auto industry. *Industrial & Labor Relations Review*, 48, 197–221.

Macky, K. and Boxall, P. 2007. The relationship between 'high-performance work practices' and employee attitudes: An investigation of additive and interaction effects. *The International Journal of Human Resource Management*, 18, 537–567.

Macky, K. and Boxall, P. 2008. High-involvement work processes, work intensification and employee well-being: A study of New Zealand worker experiences. *Asia Pacific Journal of Human Resources*, 46, 38–55.

Macneil, I. R. 1985. Relational contract: What we do and do not know. *Wisconsin Law Review*, 483–525.

Maden, C. 2015. Linking high involvement human resource practices to employee proactivity: The role of work engagement and learning goal orientation. *Personnel Review*, 44, 720–738.

Mathews, M. and Illes, K. 2015. *Leadership, trust and communication: Building trust in companies through effective communication* [Online]. Available: http://works.bepress.com/ [Accessed May 16, 2016].

Mayer, R. C. and Davis, J. H. 1999. The effect of the performance appraisal system on trust for management: A field quasi-experiment. *Journal of Applied Psychology*, 84, 123.

Mayer, R. C., Davis, J. H. and Schoorman, F. D. 1995. An integrative model of organizational trust. *Academy of Management Review*, 20, 709–734.

Mcallister, D. J. 1995. Affect-and cognition-based trust as foundations for interpersonal cooperation in organizations. *Academy of Management Journal*, 38, 24–59.

Mcevily, B., Perrone, V. and Zaheer, A. 2003. Trust as an organizing principle. *Organization Science*, 14, 91–103.

Melian-Gonzalez, S. and Verano-Tacoronte, D. 2006. Is there more than one way to manage human resources in companies? *Personnel Review*, 35, 29–50.

Messersmith, J. G. and Guthrie, J. P. 2010. High performance work systems in emergent organizations: Implications for firm performance. *Human Resource Management*, 49, 241–264.

Miles, R. E. and Snow, C. C. 2007. Organization theory and supply chain management: An evolving research perspective. *Journal of Operations Management*, 25, 459–463.

Milliken, F. J., Morrison, E. W. and Hewlin, P. F. 2003. An exploratory study of employee silence: Issues that employees don't communicate upward and why*. *Journal of Management Studies*, 40, 1453–1476.

Mishra, J. and Morrissey, M. A. 1990. Trust in employee/employer relationships: A survey of West Michigan managers. *Public Personnel Management*, 19, 443–486.

Molm, L. D. 1994. Dependence and risk: Transforming the structure of social exchange. *Social Psychology Quarterly*, 57(3), 163–176.

Moorman, R. H., Blakely, G. L. and Niehoff, B. P. 1998. Does perceived organizational support mediate the relationship between procedural justice and organizational citizenship behavior? *Academy of Management Journal*, 41, 351–357.

Morley, M., Wheeler, A. R., Coleman Gallagher, V., Brouer, R. L. and Sablynski, C. J. 2007. When person-organization (mis) fit and (dis) satisfaction lead to turnover: The moderating role of perceived job mobility. *Journal of Managerial Psychology*, 22, 203–219.

Morrison, E. W. and Milliken, F. J. 2000. Organizational silence: A barrier to change and development in a pluralistic world. *Academy of Management Review*, 25, 706–725.

Mowbray, P. K., Wilkinson, A. and Tse, H. H. M. 2015. An integrative review of employee voice: Identifying a common conceptualization and research agenda. *International Journal of Management Reviews*, 17, 382–400.

Neves, P. and Caetano, A. 2009. Commitment to change: Contributions to trust in the supervisor and work outcomes. *Group & Organization Management*, 34, 623–644.

Ng, T. W., Butts, M. M., Vandenberg, R. J., Dejoy, D. M. and Wilson, M. G. 2006. Effects of management communication, opportunity for learning, and work schedule flexibility on organizational commitment. *Journal of Vocational Behavior*, 68, 474–489.

Nishii, L. H., Lepak, D. P. and Schneider, B. 2008. Employee attributions of the "why" of HR practices: Their effects on employee attitudes and behaviors, and customer satisfaction. *Personnel Psychology*, 61, 503–545.

Oketch, M. O. 2004. The corporate stake in social cohesion. *Corporate Governance: The International Journal of Business in Society*, 4, 5–19.

Paauwe, J. 2009. HRM and performance: Achievements, methodological issues and prospects. *Journal of Management Studies*, 46, 129–142.

Park, S.-J., Kim, Y.-H., Lee, B.-K., Lee, S.-W., Lee, C. W., Hong, M.-K., Kim, J.-J., Mintz, G. S. and Park, S.-W. 2005. Sirolimus-eluting stent implantation for unprotected left main coronary artery stenosis: Comparison with bare metal stent implantation. *Journal of the American College of Cardiology*, 45, 351–356.

Pfeffer, J. 1994. Competitive advantage through people. *California Management Review*, 36, 9.

Ployhart, R. E. and Moliterno, T. P. 2011. Emergence of the human capital resource: A multilevel model. *Academy of Management Review*, 36, 127–150.

Posthuma, R. A., Campion, M. C., Masimova, M. and Campion, M. A. 2013. A high performance work practices taxonomy integrating the literature and directing future research. *Journal of Management*, 1–37.

Purcell, J. 2003. *Understanding the people and performance link: Unlocking the black box*, London: CIPD Publishing.

Purcell, J. and Hutchinson, S. 2007. Front-line managers as agents in the HRM-performance causal chain: Theory, analysis and evidence. *Human Resource Management Journal*, 17, 3–20.

Ramsay, H., Scholarios, D. and Harley, B. 2000. Employees and high-performance work systems: Testing inside the black box. *British Journal of Industrial Relations*, 38, 501–531.

Raub, S. and Robert, C. 2013. Empowerment, organizational commitment, and voice behavior in the hospitality industry evidence from a multinational sample. *Cornell Hospitality Quarterly*, 54, 136–148.

Rayton, B. A. and Yalabik, Z. Y. 2014. Work engagement, psychological contract breach and job satisfaction. *The International Journal of Human Resource Management*, 25, 2382–2400.

Renzl, B. 2008. Trust in management and knowledge sharing: The mediating effects of fear and knowledge documentation. *Omega*, 36, 206–220.

Rich, B. L., Lepine, J. A. and Crawford, E. R. 2010. Job engagement: Antecedents and effects on job performance. *Academy of Management Journal*, 53, 617–635.

Rich, G. A. 1997. The sales manager as a role model: Effects on trust, job satisfaction, and performance of salespeople. *Journal of the Academy of Marketing Science*, 25, 319–328.

Roan, A., Bramble, T. and Lafferty, G. 2001. Australian Workplace Agreements in practice: The 'hard' and 'soft' dimensions. *The Journal of Industrial Relations*, 43, 387–401.

Robinson, S. L., Kraatz, M. S. and Rousseau, D. M. 1994. Changing obligations and the psychological contract: A longitudinal study. *Academy of Management Journal*, 37, 137–152.

Rousseau, D. M. 1989. Psychological and implied contracts in organizations. *Employee Responsibilities and Rights Journal*, 2, 121–139.

Rousseau, D. M. and Greller, M. M. 1994. Human resource practices: Administrative contract makers. *Human Resource Management*, 33, 385–401.

Saks, A. M. 2006. Antecedents and consequences of employee engagement. *Journal of Managerial Psychology*, 21, 600–619.

Savery, L. K. and Luks, J. A. 2001. The relationship between empowerment, job satisfaction and reported stress levels: Some Australian evidence. *Leadership & Organization Development Journal*, 22, 97–104.

Schuler, R. S. 1991. *Managing human resources*, Eagan, MN: West publishing company.

Schuler, R. S. and Jackson, S. E. 1987. Linking competitive strategies with human resource management practices. *The Academy of Management Executive (1987–1989)*, 1(3), 207–219.

Schuler, R. S. and Macmillan, I. C. 1984. Gaining competitive advantage through human resource management practices. *Human Resource Management*, 23, 241–255.

Scott, D., Bishop, J. W. and Chen, X. 2003. An examination of the relationship of employee involvement with job satisfaction, employee cooperation, and intention to quit in US invested enterprise in China. *The International Journal of Organizational Analysis*, 11, 3–19.

Seabright, M. A., Levinthal, D. A. and Fichman, M. 1992. Role of individual attachments in the dissolution of interorganizational relationships. *Academy of Management Journal*, 35, 122–160.

Searle, R., Den Hartog, D. N., Weibel, A., Gillespie, N., Six, F., Hatzakis, T. and Skinner, D. 2011. Trust in the employer: The role of high-involvement work practices and procedural justice in European organizations. *The International Journal of Human Resource Management*, 22, 1069–1092.

Selden, S., Schimmoeller, L. and Thompson, R. 2013. The influence of high performance work systems on voluntary turnover of new hires in US state governments. *Personnel Review*, 42, 300–323.

Settoon, R. P., Bennett, N. and Liden, R. C. 1996. Social exchange in organizations: Perceived organizational support, leader–member exchange, and employee reciprocity. *Journal of Applied Psychology*, 81, 219–227.

Shaw, J. D., Dineen, B. R., Fang, R. and Vellella, R. F. 2009. Employee-organization exchange relationships, HRM practices, and quit rates of good and poor performers. *Academy of Management Journal*, 52, 1016–1033.

Sheth, J. N. 1996. Organizational buying behavior: Past performance and future expectations. *Journal of Business & Industrial Marketing*, 11, 7–24.

Shore, L. M., Tetrick, L. E., Lynch, P. and Barksdale, K. 2006. Social and economic exchange: Construct development and validation. *Journal of Applied Social Psychology*, 36, 837–867.

Shuck, B., Rocco, T. S., Truss, C., Delbridge, R., Alfes, K., Shantz, A. and Soane, E. 2014. Human resource development and employee engagement. In: Truss, C., Delbridge, R., Alfes, K., Shantz, A., and Soane, E. (eds.) *Employee Engagement in Theory and Practice*. New York: Routledge.

Snape, E. and Redman, T. 2010. HRM practices, organizational citizenship behaviour, and performance: A multi-level analysis. *Journal of Management Studies*, 47, 1219–1247.

Sparrowe, R. T. and Liden, R. C. 1997. Process and structure in leader-member exchange. *Academy of Management Review*, 22, 522–552.

Spreitzer, G. M. and Mishra, A. K. 2002. To stay or to go: Voluntary survivor turnover following an organizational downsizing. *Journal of Organizational Behavior*, 23, 707–729.

Storey, J. 1992. *Developments in the management of human resources: An analytical review*, Oxford: Blackwell.

Storey, J. 2007. *Human resource management: A critical text*, Boston, MA: Cengage Learning EMEA.

Sydow, J. 1998. Understanding the constitution of interorganizational trust. In: Lane, C and Bachmann, R (eds.) *Trust Within and Between Organizations: Conceptual Issues and Empirical Applications.* Oxford: Oxford University Press.

Tan, H. H. and Tan, C. S. 2000. Toward the differentiation of trust in supervisor and trust in organization. *Genetic, Social, and General Psychology Monographs*, 126, 241.

Tannenbaum, R. and Davis, S. A. 1969. Values, man, and organizations. In: Schmidt, W. H (ed.) *Organisational Frontiers and Human Values.* Belmont: Wadsworth..

Thibaut, J. W. and Walker, L. 1975. *Procedural justice: A psychological analysis*, Hillsdale, NJ: L. Erlbaum Associates.

Thompson, E. P. 1967. Time, work-discipline, and industrial capitalism. *Past and Present*, 38(1), 56–97.

Truss, C. 2001. Complexities and controversies in linking HRM with organizational outcomes. *Journal of Management Studies*, 38, 1121–1149.

Tyler, T. R. 1986. When does procedural justice matter in organizational settings. *Research on Negotiation in Organizations*, 1, 7–23.

Ugwu, F. O., Onyishi, I. E. and Rodríguez-Sánchez, A. M. 2014. Linking organizational trust with employee engagement: The role of psychological empowerment. *Personnel Review*, 43, 377–400.

Vandenberg, R. J., Richardson, H. A. and Eastman, L. J. 1999. The impact of high involvement work processes on organizational effectiveness a second-order latent variable approach. *Group & Organization Management*, 24, 300–339.

Van De Voorde, K. and Beijer, S. 2015. The role of employee HR attributions in the relationship between high-performance work systems and employee outcomes. *Human Resource Management Journal*, 25, 62–78.Walton, R. E. 1985. Toward a strategy of eliciting employee commitment based on policies of mutuality. In: Walton, R. E. and Lawrence, P. R. (eds.) *HRM Trends and Challenges*. Boston: Harvard Business School Press.

Wang, H., Law, K. S., Hackett, R. D., Wang, D. and Chen, Z. X. 2005. Leader-member exchange as a mediator of the relationship between transformational leadership and followers' performance and organizational citizenship behavior. *Academy of Management Journal*, 48, 420–432.

Wang, X. H. F., Fang, Y., Qureshi, I. and Janssen, O. 2015. Understanding employee innovative behavior: Integrating the social network and leader–member exchange perspectives. *Journal of Organizational Behavior*, 36, 403–420.

Way, S. A. 2002. High performance work systems and intermediate indicators of firm performance within the US small business sector. *Journal of Management*, 28, 765–785.

Wayne, S. J., Shore, L. M., Bommer, W. H. and Tetrick, L. E. 2002. The role of fair treatment and rewards in perceptions of organizational support and leader-member exchange. *Journal of Applied Psychology*, 87, 590–598.

Wayne, S. J., Shore, L. M. and Liden, R. C. 1997. Perceived organizational support and leader-member exchange: A social exchange perspective. *Academy of Management Journal*, 40, 82–111.

Whitener, E. M. 2001. Do 'high commitment' human resource practices affect employee commitment? A cross-level analysis using hierarchical linear modeling. *Journal of Management*, 27, 515–535.

Wong, Y.-T., Wong, Y.-W. and Wong, C.-S. 2015. An integrative model of turnover intention: Antecedents and their effects on employee performance in Chinese joint ventures. *Journal of Chinese Human Resource Management*, 6, 71–90.

Wood, S. J. and De Menezes, L. M. 2011. High involvement management, high-performance work systems and well-being. *The International Journal of Human Resource Management*, 22, 1586–1610.

Wood, S. J. and Wall, T. D. 2007. Work enrichment and employee voice in human resource management-performance studies. *The International Journal of Human Resource Management*, 18, 1335–1372.

Wright, B. E. and Kim, S. 2004. Participation's influence on job satisfaction the importance of job characteristics. *Review of Public Personnel Administration*, 24, 18–40.

Wright, P. M. and Boswell, W. R. 2002. Desegregating HRM: A review and synthesis of micro and macro human resource management research. *Journal of Management*, 28, 247–276.

Wright, P. M., Gardner, T. M., Moynihan, L. M. and Allen, M. R. 2005. The relationship between HR practices and firm performance: Examining causal order. *Personnel Psychology*, 58, 409–446.

Wright, P. M. and Haggerty, J. J. 2005. Missing variables in theories of strategic human resource management: Time, cause, and individuals. *Management Revue*, 16(2), 164–173.

Wright, P. M. and Mcmahan, G. C. 1992. Theoretical perspectives for strategic human resource management. *Journal of Management*, 18, 295–320.

Wright, P. M., Mcmahan, G. C. and Mcwilliams, A. 1994. Human resources and sustained competitive advantage: A resource-based perspective. *International Journal of Human Resource Management*, 5, 301–326.

Wright, P. M. and Nishii, L. 2012. Strategic human resource management and organizational behaviour: Exploring variance as an integrating framework. In: Paauwe, J., Guest, D. and Wright, P. (eds.) *HRM and Performance: Achievements and Challenges*. Chichester, UK: Wiley.

Wright, P. M. and Snell, S. A. 1998. Toward a unifying framework for exploring fit and flexibility in strategic human resource management. *Academy of Management Review*, 23, 756–772.

Wu, L., Chuang, C.-H. and Hsu, C.-H. 2014. Information sharing and collaborative behaviors in enabling supply chain performance: A social exchange perspective. *International Journal of Production Economics*, 148, 122–132.

Yang, K. and Kassekert, A. 2010. Linking management reform with employee job satisfaction: Evidence from federal agencies. *Journal of Public Administration Research and Theory*, 20, 413–436.

Yijing, L. and Yong, S. 2015. Can authentic leadership break employee silence? A moderated mediation model. *Journal of Psychological Science*, 5, 23–49.

Yousef, D. A. 1998. Satisfaction with job security as a predictor of organizational commitment and job performance in a multicultural environment. *International Journal of Manpower*, 19, 184–194.

Yun, S., Takeuchi, R. and Liu, W. 2007. Employee self-enhancement motives and job performance behaviors: Investigating the moderating effects of employee role ambiguity and managerial perceptions of employee commitment. *Journal of Applied Psychology*, 92, 745–756.

Zacharatos, A., Barling, J. and Iverson, R. D. 2005. High-performance work systems and occupational safety. *Journal of Applied Psychology*, 90, 77–93.

Zhou, J. and George, J. M. 2001. When job dissatisfaction leads to creativity: Encouraging the expression of voice. *Academy of Management Journal*, 44, 682–696.

Zucker, L. G. 1986. Production of trust: Institutional sources of economic structure, 1840–1920. *Research in Organizational Behavior*, 8, 53–111.

3 SHRM/HPWS in China and case study profiles

Introduction

A review of SHRM/HPWS studies from Western literature tells us how SHRM/HPWS are explored in the West. These studies cover a number of aspects, such as relationships between HR practices and organizational performance, relationships between HR practices and employee outcomes and contextual factors affecting the implementation of SHRM/HPWS. As China opens to changes, opportunities and challenges under the 'open door' policy, Western ideas have been introduced into China, and Chinese managers have been adopting them in the workplace. This trend has generated interest in how SHRM/HPWS have been implemented in a different environment with different political, economic, historical and social/culture backgrounds. It is also expected that managers in China might have their own rationale for selecting certain aspects of SHRM/HPWS in order to adapt these to the situation in China.

This chapter starts by focusing on the current SHRM/HPWS research and publications in China. Attention then shifts to introducing our research in detail, which includes our selection of SOEs and DPEs from among the Chinese indigenous enterprise ownership models, our research design (using a mixed-method of both qualitative and quantitative analysis), interviewee profiles and survey targets, as well as an explanation of our interview questions and the survey questionnaire. A relatively comprehensive picture of our fieldwork and case studies is presented before a detailed discussion of the research results in chapters 4 and 5.

SHRM/HPWS studies in China

Studies in recent years on SHRM/HPWS have expanded their scope beyond the historical focus on the US and Western systems. A number of research projects have tested the applicability of SHRM in other social/cultural environments. For example, research has been carried out in Spain (Martin-Tapia et al., 2009), Singapore (Wu and Chaturvedi, 2009), Taiwan (Chuang and Liao, 2010), Japan (Takeuchi et al., 2009), New Zealand (Fabling and Grimes, 2010) and China (Gong et al., 2010; Qiao et al., 2009; Shih et al., 2013).

Faced with unprecedented changes in social, cultural, legal and institutional environments, Chinese enterprises have made efforts to adopt and implement SHRM/HPWS (Cooke, 2005; Warner, 2004; Zhu et al., 2007). It is shown that SHRM is flourishing and practiced in a range of organizations, including indigenous enterprises, namely SOEs and DPEs (Warner, 2004). Therefore, it is not surprising to find that research relevant to SHRM in China attracts the attention of scholars. According to Qiao et al. (2009), studies in the Chinese context have covered the same three primary streams as those in Western studies. The first stream explores convergent, divergent and cross-vergent aspects of HR practices (Warner, 1993; Zhu and Dowling, 2002); the second focuses on strategic orientation of HRM (Hu et al., 2015; Law et al., 2003); the third stream considers SHRM/HPWS and employee reaction (Chen, 1995; Zhang and Morris, 2014).

Studies in the first two streams present rich analyses. They support the applicability of SHRM with Chinese characteristics (Cooke, 2005). For example, Björkman and Xiucheng (2002) demonstrated that the SHRM index was significantly and positively related to firm performance measured by using foreign invested companies in China. Zheng et al. (2006) showed that SHRM was positively associated with HR outcomes in small and medium sized enterprises in China. Zhang and Morris (2014) observed that HPWS positively impact on performance among different ownership enterprises in China. In contrast to the extensive discussion in the first two streams, the third stream is rarely addressed by studies. In the Western literature, employees' perspectives attract relatively little attention (Guest, 2002). It is not surprising to find even fewer studies on employees' perspectives in the context of China.

A number of publications have appeared in recent years on HPWS within the context of China. For example, Sun et al. (2007) demonstrated that HPWS were positively associated with employee retention and productivity. Glover and Siu (2000) suggested that high wages, extensive training and internal career planning were necessary for Chinese firms to effectively manage product quality. Similar studies such as those conducted by Wei and Lau (2005) and Wang et al. (2007) also support the correlation of HPWS with improved performance. However, few studies within the context of China have included employees' perspectives in their HPWS studies. Shih et al. (2013) included employee-perceived HPWS practices in their studies. They targeted employees who worked in China for multinational corporations with headquarters in Taiwan. Qiao et al. (2009) examined employees' experiences with HPWS and their commitment in manufacturing companies. Zhang et al. (2013) demonstrated the effects of HPWS on employees' well-being in Chinese hospitals. So far, there has been no substantial research on HPWS in China from the employees' perspectives. A recent study by Cooke et al. (2016) investigated the relationship between HPWS and employee resilience and engagement. These researchers suggested that HPWS positively affected resilience and engagement. Another study conducted by Jiang et al. (2015) discussed the contextual influence of managers and co-workers on employees' perceptions of HR practices. Based on these research publications, it is clear that the gap in research on the adoption and implementation of SHRM/

HPWS from both managerial and employees' perspectives should be addressed, thus the focus of our research.

Enterprise ownership in China HRM studies

In recent years, more effort has been made to understand the cultural and historical influences on HR practices in China (Warner, 2004), providing guidance to multinational companies operating in China. HPWS were introduced and implemented in many Western multinational companies (Zhu et al., 2005). With this introduction of HPWS, many Chinese domestic enterprises began to embrace the concept of HPWS (Zhu and Warner, 2004). Moreover, education systems such as MBA programs and translated textbooks intensified the impact of HPWS on Chinese indigenous enterprises (Warner, 2004).

Although it is claimed that Chinese indigenous enterprises have widely adopted HPWS, little research has been found to assess differential adoption of HPWS by different ownership types in China (Wang et al., 2007). Moreover, it is suggested that performance differs by types of enterprise implementing HPWS (Law et al., 2003). Various types of ownership and organizational supports might lead to the different adoption of HPWS with different outcomes (Zhu and Warner, 2004)

Therefore, the intention of this book is to target the HPWS in Chinese indigenous enterprises, namely SOEs and DPEs. Both enterprise types are characterized as Chinese indigenous enterprises with relatively low influence of Western management theory, in comparison with foreign multinational companies, joint ventures and foreign invested enterprises. By focusing on SOEs and DPEs, the present book intends to understand HPWS from both managerial and employees' perspectives in Chinese companies with specific indigenous insight.

Historically, HRM in Chinese SOEs has been dominated by a traditional personnel administration system (Warner and Ying, 1998). Under this traditional system, enterprises have not had autonomy to make HR-related decisions, which are normally controlled by government (Zhu and Warner, 2004). Nowadays, China has been largely transformed into a market economy, and SOEs have been reformed. However, they are still characterized by some traditional personnel administration features. For example, HR practices are controlled by top management or regional senior officials. SOEs are required to provide service to the public instead of purely making profit (Ding and Warner, 2001; Lewis, 2003; Ngo et al., 2014). While SOEs have been transforming gradually, DPEs have grown quickly, and they also have adopted SHRM/HPWS as their new HRM policies and practices. They hire capable HR managers who have experience in managing people and are capable of implementing new ideas and systems. DPEs have developed advanced HR practices in order to outperform their competitors (Law et al., 2003; Qiao et al., 2015). Therefore, it is worthwhile to compare the status of SHRM/HPWS among these two types of indigenous enterprises (Ding and Warner, 2001; Lewis, 2003).

In summary, HPWS in the context of China have attracted the attention of scholars. We have chosen SOEs and DPEs with the expectation of demonstrating

HPWS with certain Chinese characteristics. Additionally, this study investigates employee perceptions of HPWS and its effects on employee outcomes in order to confirm the criticism of the managerial orientation in mainstream HPWS studies.

Research design

In this research, we adopt a mixed method in order to explore the applicability of Western theories in the context of Chinese enterprises and tackle the research gaps identified earlier by testing the relevant unknown issues using appropriate methods suggested by Blaikie (1995). In the first stage of the qualitative study, in-depth interviews were conducted to obtain detailed and explorative information to address the emerging phenomena of HPWS with an emphasis on both managerial and employees' views. A collection of well-grounded, rich descriptions and explanations of processes from both managers and employees (Miles and Huberman, 1994) assists in explicating the HPWS phenomena and identifying the SHRM/HPWS elements being implemented in SOEs and DPEs, as well as how these influence the realization of business goals and employees' attitudes and behaviours. Following the first stage of explorative study, survey questionnaires were designed, survey target companies and individuals were selected and survey questionnaires were distributed among them. The following section provides detailed information about these two-stage research activities.

Stage One study

Given the emerging nature of the concept of HPWS in China as well as the inadequacies in understanding this system, a flexible strategy of enquiry was necessary to provide efficient communication to collect data and investigate meanings (Easterby-Smith, 1986). In the Stage One study, semi-structured interviews were employed. This method derives benefits from the standardization and flexibility to explore an area partly unexplained. It is also a powerful tool to discover the complexity and subtlety of issues. It enables the researcher to obtain rich and detailed information from interviewees and to have better control over interview questions (Creswell et al., 2003).

Two rounds of qualitative empirical work were undertaken in the Stage One study. The first round involved two focus group discussions conducted in the Fujian province of China. These provided a useful opportunity to pilot test the structure of the interview questions. Each focus group discussion lasted approximately one hour. In total, nine participants joined the pilot test; three were HR managers, and the rest were ordinary employees. The average age of the three HR managers was 35, and the average job tenure with their current employer was five years. The average age of the employees was 29, and the average job tenure with their current employer was two years. Male and female employees were equally represented (i.e., three male and three female employees).

Subsequently, the interview questions were further revised and refined based on suggestions made by participants in the pilot study. After the interview questions were confirmed (see Appendices I [managers] and II [employees]) for the interview questions), we selected our targets using a random purposeful sampling strategy (Miles and Huberman, 1994). Companies were randomly selected from the most developed cities in China, including Hangzhou, Fuzhou, Xiamen and Guangzhou. Hangzhou is the capital city of Zhejiang province in Eastern China; Fuzhou and Xiamen are the most developed cities in Fujian province, one being the provincial capital city and another one of the Special Economic Zones in southeast China; Guangzhou is the capital city of Guangdong province in Southern China. These cities were chosen because they represent high levels of economic development with high levels of exposure to Western managerial concepts, such as SHRM/HPWS, providing us with the relevant information required for this research project.

We identified our targets by selecting SOEs and DPEs in each city from the local telephone directory. The researchers communicated with these companies' HR managers and requested permission from top management to interview HR managers and employees. An email was sent to all potential participants with an explanation of the research, ensuring that participation was voluntary and that confidentiality was protected. We obtained agreement from 51 participants, including 11 HR managers and 40 employees from four SOEs and seven DPEs (see Table 3.1). Among the 11 HR managers who participated in the interviews, four were from SOEs and seven were from DPEs. All HR managers were employed full time; their average age was about 39 years (SOEs) and 38 years (DPEs), and average job tenure in their current position was about 11 years (SOEs) and 7 years (DPEs). The employee participants consisted of 40 individuals, and 13 of the interviews were conducted in SOEs. The average age was about 28 years, and average job tenure in the current positions was about three years. The interviews in the DPEs were held with 27 employees, with an average age of 23 years and average job tenure of two years. All interviews were undertaken in locations convenient to the participants, predominately in their workplace. Each interview lasted approximately one to one and one-half hours.

One issue which needs to be addressed here is the imbalance in the number of the sampled companies between SOEs and DPEs. Since the reform on SOEs in the mid-1990s, a large number of former SOEs have been corporatized and privatized, and nowadays only 110 centrally controlled SOEs and another 80,000 provincial and local government controlled SOEs exist (Cendrowski, 2015). The Chinese economy is supplemented by the increasing number of DPEs and the competition generated by these enterprises (Warner and Zhu, 2010). The number of DPEs is approximately 1,250,000 in China (China Private Enterprises Year Book, 2014). The relatively small number of SOEs limits the scale of sampling in this study. It is admitted that a balanced design of SOE and DPE samples provides greater analytical power than an imbalanced design. However, given the lower number of SOEs available, it is difficult to achieve total balance between the selected number of SOEs and DPEs. Therefore, this research also reflects the current reality of ownership in China where the traditional dominant SOEs

Table 3.1 Interviewee profiles

Interviewee ID	*Gender*	*Age*	*Occupation*	*Education level*	*Years with current employer*
SOE1M1	M	38	Manager	Master	5
SOE1E1	M	23	Marketing Specialist	Bachelor	1
SOE1E2	F	27	Admin Staff	Bachelor	3
SOE1E3	M	33	Technician	Master	2
SOE2M1	F	42	Manager	Bachelor	16
SOE2E1	M	23	Operational Staff	High School	5
SOE2E2	M	30	Technician	Master	3
SOE2E3	F	33	HR Specialist	Bachelor	3
SOE2E4	F	22	Accountant	Bachelor	0.5
SOE3M1	F	35	Manager	Bachelor	10
SOE2E1	M	28	Technician	Bachelor	7
SOE3E2	F	21	Admin Staff	High School	1
SOE3E3	M	26	Technician	Bachelor	3
SOE4M1	M	40	Manager	Bachelor	11
SOE4E1	M	31	Admin Staff	Bachelor	6
SOE4E2	F	27	HR Specialist	Master	0.5
SOE4E3	F	36	Technician	Master	5
DPE1M1	M	46	Manager	Bachelor	15
DPE1E1	M	30	HR Specialist	Bachelor	10
DPE1E2	F	23	Marketing Specialist	High School	2
DPE1E3	M	22	Admin Staff	Bachelor	1
DPE2M1	M	42	Manager	Bachelor	10
DPE2E1	M	23	Technician	Bachelor	1
DPE2E2	M	22	Technician	Bachelor	1
DPE2E3	F	20	Operational Staff	High School	2
DPE2E4	M	21	Marketing Specialist	High School	2
DPE2E5	F	25	Marketing Specialist	High School	2
DPE3M1	F	33	Manager	Bachelor	5
DPE3E1	F	19	Operational Staff	High School	1
DPE3E2	M	19	Operational Staff	High School	1
DPE3E3	M	19	Operational Staff	High School	1
DPE3E4	F	22	Operational Staff	High School	3
DPE4M1	F	35	Manager	Master	3
DPE4E1	M	22	Operational Staff	High School	2
DPE4E2	F	22	Operational Staff	High School	2

Interviewee ID	*Gender*	*Age*	*Occupation*	*Education level*	*Years with current employer*
DEP4E4	F	22	Operational Staff	High School	1
DPE4E5	M	25	Marketing Specialist	Bachelor	1
DPE5M1	M	36	Manager	Master	8
DPE5E1	F	22	Operational Staff	High School	3
DPE5E2	M	23	Operational Staff	High School	5
DPE5E3	F	20	Operational Staff	High School	0.5
DPE6M1	F	38	Manager	Bachelor	5
DPE6E1	F	27	Technician	Bachelor	2
DPE6E2	M	28	Technician	Bachelor	2
DPE6E3	F	23	Marketing Specialist	Bachelor	2
DPE6E4	F	29	Accountant	Bachelor	3
DPE7M1	M	39	Manager	Bachelor	2
DPE7E1	M	24	Technician	Bachelor	1
DPE7E2	F	25	HR Specialist	Bachelor	1
DPE7E3	F	23	Admin Staff	Bachelor	1

Notes: SOE1M1 = manager 1 from SOE1; SOE1E1 = employee 1 from SOE1; DPE1M1 = manager 1 from DPE1; DPE1E1 = employee 1 from DPE1
F = female; M = male

Source: based on authors' interviews (January 2013)

have been declining and more newly established DPEs have been emerging, thus changing the economic landscape in China.

Stage Two study

The Stage Two study was designed as quantitative research based on the knowledge gained in the Stage One qualitative research. The second stage measured and tested our hypotheses and explored the mediating effect of manager–employee trust relationships between the implementation of HPWS and employees' outcomes (job satisfaction and commitment).

The questionnaire was developed based on an extensive literature review and confirmed by the interviews and pilot studies of Stage One of this research. Translation and back-translation techniques were used to enhance the reliability and validity of the questionnaires (Chen and Boore, 2010). The questionnaires were originally drafted in English and then translated into Chinese by the researcher, who is bilingual in Chinese and English. Back translation was conducted by two academics who were also bilingual and worked in a major Chinese university (Brislin, 1980).

A pilot test was undertaken by 20 employees prior to distributing questionnaires. The employees were requested to evaluate the questionnaires in terms of instructions and wording. Specifically, they were invited to assess: a) time to finish the questionnaire; b) ease of the questions; c) missing items; d) unclear items; and e) comments on improving the questionnaires. The pilot study confirmed the appropriateness of questions for employees in Chinese indigenous enterprises, although minor adjustments were made according to participants' suggestions (see Appendix III survey questionnaires [employees]).

This book pays particular attention to the perspectives of employees regarding the implementation of HPWS, and their job satisfaction and commitment, supported by survey data collected from employees working in SOEs and DPEs. Since we had completed the first round of selection of our target SOEs and DPEs in the four developed cities mentioned earlier, we continued to work with those companies in Stage One of our study, at the same time expanding the range of target companies in the same locations to ensure consistency with the case studies identified for Stage One of the research. The selection of the survey targets was based on the following criteria: at least four companies (two SOEs and two DPEs) were to be chosen in each location, and at least one large size (over 500 employees) and one medium or small size (less than 300 employees) company was to be chosen from each ownership category. Companies from different industries were included. In each sampled company, stratified random sampling was conducted with the employee participants. Profiles of the sampled organizations are listed in Table 3.2.

In total, 1,100 questionnaires were sent out, and 956 completed questionnaires were returned, reflecting a response rate of approximately 86 percent. This sample size is acceptable for performing a structural equation modelling statistical analysis. As a rule of thumb, a sample size of 200 is considered the minimum for SEM analysis. Bentler and Chou (1987) suggested that the ratio of sample size to the number of free parameters should be at least 5:1. In this research, 261 responses were from SOEs, and 695 were from DPEs, with 67 percent of employees being male, and the average age 29 (see more detailed target profile in Table 3.3).

Based on the aforementioned research design, we could carry out further investigation in line with our key research questions and hypotheses. In the following chapters, namely chapters 4 and 5, we will provide more detailed information on the elaboration of our interview results and the consequent implications, as well as our survey results, before generating meaningful discussion and conclusion in chapter 6.

Conclusion

With rapid changes in China, Chinese enterprises face unprecedented challenges and opportunities. In order to deal with these, management in Chinese enterprises adopt a number of so-called 'advanced HR practices'. Their adoption and implementation of SHRM/HPWS demonstrate some commonalities with their

Table 3.2 Survey target organization profiles

Company ID	*Location*	*Number of employees*	*Industry*
SOE1	Hangzhou	1,000	Manufacturing
SOE2	Hangzhou	380	Insurance
SOE3	Fuzhou	1,000	Energy
SOE4	Fuzhou	150	Construction
SOE5	Xiamen	3,000	Energy
SOE6	Xiamen	110	Tourism
SOE7	Guangzhou	550	Construction
SOE8	Guangzhou	200	Construction
DPE1	Hangzhou	2,500	Manufacturing-Textile
DPE2	Hangzhou	800	Property Management
DPE3	Hangzhou	80	Export
DPE4	Fuzhou	3,000	IT
DPE5	Fuzhou	156	Electrics
DPE6	Fuzhou	140	Retail (Automatic)
DPE7	Fuzhou	165	IT
DPE8	Fuzhou	300	Manufacturing-Auto parts
DPE9	Fuzhou	400	Manufacturing-Furniture
DPD10	Fuzhou	120	Hotel
DPE11	Xiamen	1,200	Transport
DPE12	Xiamen	100	Refinery-Petrochemical
DPE13	Xiamen	80	Retail and Export
DPE14	Xiamen	350	IT
DPE15	Xiamen	30	After Sale Service-Auto
DPE16	Guangzhou	212	Real Estate
DPE17	Guangzhou	350	Manufacturing-Elevator
DPE18	Guangzhou	2,000	Property Management
DPE19	Guangzhou	25	Graphic Design
DPE20	Guangzhou	50	Software Development

Source: based on authors' surveys (November 2014 and January 2015)

Western counterparts, as well as some unique 'Chinese Characteristics' (Warner, 2004). Given the importance of China and the sparsity of SHRM/HPWS studies in China, focusing on two types of Chinese indigenous enterprises (i.e., SOEs and DPEs) is expected to further understanding of SHRM/HPWS implementation in China.

Since relevant studies are few, the purpose of this book is predominately exploratory in nature. It seeks qualitative data and confirmed applicability of the

Table 3.3 Profiles of employee participants

Demographic characteristics	*Number of employees (N)*	*Percentage (%)*
Gender		
Male	641	67.05
Female	315	32.95
Age (years)		
Less than 25	477	49.90
25–35	324	33.89
More than 35	155	16.21
Education background		
High school and equivalent	201	21.03
Bachelor	489	51.15
Master and above	266	27.82
Ownership		
SOEs	261	27.30
DPEs	695	72.70

Source: based on authors' surveys (November 2014 and January 2015)

proposed research framework and identifies any unknown issues. A quantitative study was undertaken to test the impact of current prevalent HPWS on employee job satisfaction and commitment. The results of this study are timely and significant in understanding changes in practices and their impact on indigenous Chinese enterprises.

References

Bentler, P. M. and Chou, C.-P. 1987. Practical issues in structural modeling. *Sociological Methods & Research*, 16, 78–117.

Björkman, I. and Xiucheng, F. 2002. Human resource management and the performance of Western firms in China. *International Journal of Human Resource Management*, 13, 853–864.

Blaikie, P. 1995. Changing environments or changing views? A political ecology for developing countries. *Geography: Journal of the Geographical Association*, 80, 203–214.

Brislin, R. W. 1980. Translation and content analysis of oral and written material. *Handbook of Cross-Cultural Psychology*, 2, 349–444.

Cendrowski, S. 2015. *Why China's SOE reform would always disappoint* [Online]. Available: http://fortune.com/2015/09/15/why-chinas-soe-reform-would-always-disappoint/ [Accessed March 12 2016].

Chen, C. C. 1995. New trends in rewards allocation preferences: A Sino-US comparison. *Academy of Management Journal*, 38, 408–428.

Chen, H. Y. and Boore, J. R. 2010. Translation and back-translation in qualitative nursing research: Methodological review. *Journal of Clinical Nursing*, 19, 234–239.

China Private Enterprises Year Book 2014. *China private enterprises year book*. Beijing: All-China Federation of Industry and Commerce Press.

Chuang, C.-H. and Liao, H. 2010. Strategic human resource management in service context: Taking care of business by taking care of employees and customers. *Personnel Psychology*, 63, 153–196.

Cooke, F. L. 2005. *HRM, work and employment in China*, Hove: Psychology Press.

Cooke, F. L., Cooper, B., Bartram, T., Wang, J. and Mei, H. 2016. Mapping the relationships between high-performance work systems, employee resilience and engagement: A study of the banking industry in China. *The International Journal of Human Resource Management*, 1, 1–22.

Creswell, J. W., Plano Clark, V. L., Gutmann, M. L. and Hanson, W. E. 2003. Advanced mixed methods research designs. In: Tashakkori, A. and Teddlie, C. (eds.) *Handbook of Mixed Methods in Social and Behavioral Research*. Thousand Oaks, CA: Sage.

Ding, D. Z. and Warner, M. 2001. China's labour-management system reforms: Breaking the 'Three Old Irons'(1978–1999). *Asia Pacific Journal of Management*, 18, 315–334.

Easterby-Smith, M. 1986. *Evaluating management education, training and development*, Farnham: Gower Publishing Company.

Fabling, R. and Grimes, A. 2010. HR practices and New Zealand firm performance: What matters and who does it? *The International Journal of Human Resource Management*, 21, 488–508.

Glover, L. and Siu, N. 2000. The human resource barriers to managing quality in China. *International Journal of Human Resource Management*, 11, 867–882.

Gong, Y., Chang, S. and Cheung, S. Y. 2010. High performance work system and collective OCB: A collective social exchange perspective. *Human Resource Management Journal*, 20, 119–137.

Guest, D. 2002. Human resource management, corporate performance and employee wellbeing: Building the worker into HRM. *Journal of Industrial Relations*, 44, 335–358.

Hu, H., Wu, J. and Shi, J. 2015. Strategic HRM and organisational learning in the Chinese private sector during second-pioneering. *The International Journal of Human Resource Management*, 27, 1813–1832.

Jiang, K., Hu, J., Liu, S. and Lepak, D. P. 2015. Understanding employees' perceptions of human resource practices: Effects of demographic dissimilarity to managers and coworkers. *Human Resource Management*, 10, 1–23.

Law, K. S., Tse, D. and Zhou, N. 2003. Does human resource management matter in a transitional economy? China as an example. *Journal of International Business Studies*, 34, 255–265.

Lewis, P. 2003. New China-old ways? A case study of the prospects for implementing human resource management practices in a Chinese state-owned enterprise. *Employee Relations*, 25, 42–60.

Martin-Tapia, I., Aragon-Correa, J. A. and Guthrie, J. P. 2009. High performance work systems and export performance. *The International Journal of Human Resource Management*, 20, 633–653.

Miles, M. B. and Huberman, A. M. 1994. *Qualitative data analysis: An expanded sourcebook*, London: Sage.

Ngo, H.-Y., Jiang, C.-Y. and Loi, R. 2014. Linking HRM competency to firm performance: An empirical investigation of Chinese firms. *Personnel Review*, 43, 898–914.

Qiao, K., Khilji, S. and Wang, X. 2009. High-performance work systems, organizational commitment, and the role of demographic features in the people's republic of China. *The International Journal of Human Resource Management*, 20, 2311–2330.

Qiao, K., Wang, X. and Wei, L. Q. 2015. Determinants of high-performance work systems in small and medium-sized private enterprises in China. *Asia Pacific Journal of Human Resources*, 53, 185–203.

Shih, H.-A., Chiang, Y.-H. and Hsu, C.-C. 2013. High performance work system and HCN performance. *Journal of Business Research*, 66, 540–546.

Sun, L.-Y., Aryee, S. and Law, K. S. 2007. High-performance human resource practices, citizenship behavior, and organizational performance: A relational perspective. *Academy of Management Journal*, 50, 558–577.

Takeuchi, R., Chen, G. and Lepak, D. P. 2009. Through the looking glass of a social system: Cross-level effects of high-performance work systems on employees' attitudes. *Personnel Psychology*, 62, 1–29.

Wang, X., Bruning, N. S. and Peng, S. 2007. Western high-performance HR practices in China: A comparison among public-owned, private and foreign-invested enterprises. *The International Journal of Human Resource Management*, 18, 684–701.

Warner, M. 1993. Human resource management 'with Chinese characteristics'. *International Journal of Human Resource Management*, 4, 45–65.

Warner, M. 2004. Human resource management in China revisited: Introduction. *The International Journal of Human Resource Management*, 15, 617–634.

Warner, M. and Ying, Z. 1998. Re-assessing Chinese management: The influence of indigenous versus exogenous models. *Human Systems Management*, 17, 245–255.

Warner, M. and Zhu, Y. 2010. Labour and management in the people's republic of China: Seeking the 'harmonious society'. *Asia Pacific Business Review*, 16, 285–298.

Wei, L.-Q. and Lau, C.-M. 2005. Market orientation, HRM importance and competency: Determinants of strategic HRM in Chinese firms. *The International Journal of Human Resource Management*, 16, 1901–1918.

Wu, P.-C. and Chaturvedi, S. 2009. The role of procedural justice and power distance in the relationship between high performance work systems and employee attitudes: A multilevel perspective. *Journal of Management*, 35, 1228–1247.

Zhang, B. and Morris, J. L. 2014. High-performance work systems and organizational performance: Testing the mediation role of employee outcomes using evidence from PR China. *The International Journal of Human Resource Management*, 25, 68–90.

Zhang, M., Zhu, C. J., Dowling, P. J. and Bartram, T. 2013. Exploring the effects of high-performance work systems (HPWS) on the work-related well-being of Chinese hospital employees. *The International Journal of Human Resource Management*, 24, 3196–3212.

Zheng, C., Morrison, M. and O'neill, G. 2006. An empirical study of high performance HRM practices in Chinese SMEs. *The International Journal of Human Resource Management*, 17, 1772–1803.

Zhu, C. J., Cooper, B., De Cieri, H. and Dowling, P. J. 2005. A problematic transition to a strategic role: Human resource management in industrial enterprises in China. *The International Journal of Human Resource Management*, 16, 513–531.

Zhu, C. J. and Dowling, P. J. 2002. Staffing practices in transition: Some empirical evidence from China. *International Journal of Human Resource Management*, 13, 569–597.

Zhu, Y. and Warner, M. 2004. Changing patterns of human resource management in contemporary China: WTO accession and enterprise responses. *Industrial Relations Journal*, 35(4), 311–328.

Zhu, Y., Warner, M. and Rowley, C. 2007. Human resource management with 'Asian' characteristics: A hybrid people-management system in East Asia. *The International Journal of Human Resource Management*, 18, 745–768.

4 Implementation of SHRM/HPWS in SOEs and DPEs

Introduction

Previous chapters reviewed the theoretical framework underpinning this study and outlined the factors impacting the transformation of HRM and SHRM in China. This chapter investigates the relationships between SHRM policies and practices and employee outcomes, addressing a number of key research questions, namely: 1) What are the manager and employee perspectives of the SHRM/HPWS adopted and implemented in China? 2) What insights can we gain of SHRM and HPWS in SOEs and DPEs in China? 3) What HRM systems can organizations develop to encourage positive attitudes of employees? 4) What direction should managers and organizations take in implementing strategies for HRM and HPWS?

By linking and comparing managers' and employees' responses, this chapter draws a relatively comprehensive picture of the adoption and implementation of HPWS at the organizational level in Chinese indigenous companies from both 'top-down' and 'bottom-up' perspectives. This study attempts to close the gap in current literature, which focuses more on managerial perspectives than on employees' perspectives, as well as lacks comparative studies between the two groups.

This chapter first presents the research context, followed by managerial and employees' responses to the adoption and implementation of SHRM/HPWS, and concludes by highlighting a number of meaningful implications.

Research context

Strategic HR practices transformed from HRM to SHRM systems are linked to business strategies; they are aligned with other HR policies and practices horizontally. Bundles of practices effectively affect general performance rather than individual practice (Armstrong et al., 2010). HPWS are a set of HR practices characterized by employees' participation and a positive relationship with performance (Lawler, 1986).

Initially, HPWS represent a managerial orientation approach that offers opportunities for employees to become involved (Lawler III, 1986). Previous studies show that HPWS result in positive outcomes in areas such as financial performance (Bae and Lawler, 2000; Evans and Davis, 2005; Huselid, 1995), operational performance (Guthrie, 2001; Ichniowski and Shaw, 1999), occupational safety (Zacharatos et al., 2005) and a high level of motivation and commitment (Gould-Williams, 2003; Whitener, 2001).

As noted, efforts have been made to explore the HPWS–performance relationship, focusing on the influence of management. This is identified by Appelbaum and Batt (1994) as a 'top-down' approach; in contrast, they proposed an employee-centric 'bottom-up' approach. The 'bottom-up' approach recognizes the importance of employees, suggesting that employees' interests, experience and perceptions possibly affect HPWS implementation.

This research incorporates employee outcomes and employee perceptions in the proposed research model based on the study by Guest and Conway (2002). Managers and employees were interviewed in the qualitative study stage. They were invited to answer questions about the same issues in order to identify similarities and differences between the groups. On the one hand, managers' interpretations of HR are related to those of employees because managers' interpretations provide the context within which employees form their perceptions (Liao et al., 2009). Manager perceptions of HR practices are not necessarily the same as employees' because people perceive reality differently due to their different viewpoints (e.g., educational background, age group, occupation and position). Differences between individual interpretations within the employee group are expected in this research. According to social exchange literature, employees respond differently to the same HR practices (Lepak and Snell, 2002).

Managers' responses

A company's management decision-making process usually takes place at its top level, with a strategic planning group consisting of the chief executive officers, the chief financial officers, the president and various directors. Managers' responses are examined in this section in order to illustrate how HPWS is adopted and implemented in Chinese indigenous companies. Realizing the importance of employee participation, most managers in SOEs and DPEs made a great effort to involve employees in the entire process of adoption and implementation of HPWS. Practices adopted to encourage employee participation demonstrated different characteristics of management, directional strategies and internal labour structure.

Staffing

Staffing has many implications for organizations. Nowadays, many organizations are dealing with skills shortages and difficulties in attracting and retaining talent. The goal of staffing is more than simply generating large numbers of applicants. Rather, the objective is to ensure that the organization has a pool of qualified applicants who would accept a job when a vacancy occurs.

In order to achieve the strategic goals of the organization, it is necessary to translate strategic goals into human resource policies and practices. In terms of staffing, human resources planning helps ensure that future business goals (e.g., financial objectives, production goals and technological advancement) are fulfilled with the right number of employees and the appropriate skills. According to the interview results with managers, general practices regarding the process of staffing start with the determination of the current supply of and demand for labour and the prediction of future labour shortages or surpluses within organizations. When vacancies occur or are newly created, the specific requirements of knowledge, skill, ability and other personal characteristics for these vacancies are developed and documented. The importance of planning in order to implement business strategies is addressed by all HR managers from both SOEs and DPEs. They agree that staff planning should be conducted prior to initiating recruitment and that this process should be aligned with a number of factors within organizations.

According to the managers' responses, the factors considered can be classified into the following categories. The first factor is business strategy, which identifies certain skills, knowledge and characteristics. Analysis of the overall labour market situation (i.e., labour supply and demand), especially future supply and demand, is carried out. Once this analysis has been conducted, the skills, knowledge and characteristics which fit the business strategy are identified. Such skills, knowledge and characteristics are included in job descriptions and are used as a guide in recruitment interviews. A number of sampled companies have adopted such practices. For example, the manager from DPE2 said: 'Innovation is the powerhouse of our company, even if it is very difficult to tell whether applicants are creative or not during interviews. It is a characteristic which is listed in our job description and screened in interviews'. In fact, company culture is a factor considered in planning among the majority of sampled companies. Managers agreed that employee fit in terms of organizational culture affects employees' commitment to the organization.

In the managers' opinion, staffing is more than finding qualified employees to fill vacancies; its scope extends to finding qualified employees who not only accept the job, but also stay with their employers for the long term. In this sense, acceptance and fitting in with organizational culture are important, as implied by brochures distributed to applicants. One manager stated: 'Harmony and respect is the central theme of our culture. We emphasize the importance of showing respect to parents, colleagues, clients and suppliers' (DPE1M1). Staffing is perceived as having a long-term orientation.

As the business develops the demand for staff fluctuates so managers must tackle the problem of how to re-allocate redundant skills. One possible solution is a long-term planning perspective. For example, the manager from SOE2 said: 'The majority of positions recruited in our company is continuing; we need to be cautious as we are not able to lay them off if demand for a particular job is temporary. In other words, we aim to recruit employees to fulfil our short-term demand, but more importantly, to fulfil long-term demand'. In addition, the external economic environment is an important issue, and economic booms or crises and maintaining market share guide recruitment numbers. Generally speaking, based on these managers' views, employee participation is not common in staff planning either in SOEs or in DPEs. The underlying reason for not involving employees is the complexity of planning; it requires access to information and a thorough understanding of the company, which most employees do not have. The manager from SOE2 said: 'We have more than 1,000 employees and the organizational structure is complicated. For example, our organization consists of five sub-companies which oversee supplying, maintaining and repairing works in five districts in this city. Each sub-company has offices or branches. We have a factory on the outskirts of this city. It is extremely difficult for ordinary employees to identify the demand for jobs and then to get involved in the process. Managers have clearer views of the whole picture than employees do'. According to the managers, another factor to consider is that employee involvement in planning is not practical and cost efficient. Although managers agreed that employee involvement provides perspectives for identifying demand and supply within the company, managers carry the responsibility for expenses. According to the manager from DPE3: 'Involving employees in job planning is not practical. If we collect all employees' opinions, it is costly and time consuming. If we just collect some of the employees' opinions, we get complaints that it is not fair and representative'.

An exception to employee involvement in planning is team leader participation. In contrast to ordinary employees, team leaders have supervisory responsibility and tend to be knowledgeable and capable of identifying skills shortages at work, especially in the areas in which they have expertise; therefore, involving them in the process of planning helps achieve strategic goals. Compared with collecting employee opinions, the ideas and views of team leaders are considered to be informative, practical and cost efficient. The manager from SOE3 said: 'When we are creating new jobs, opinions from team leaders are collected as they are supposed to know better about what skills we need than these senior managers do'.

Another aspect of staffing is talent sourcing, which is normally perceived by managers as the responsibility of the HR department. The managers interviewed used a number of strategies to attract or identify candidates to fill job vacancies. They used internal and/or external advertising; appropriate media, such as local or national newspapers; specialist recruitment media; professional publications; window advertisements; and a variety of internet options. There were similarities in SOEs and DPEs in the methods they used to source talent. The choice of methods reflects the characteristics of management and the company. To be specific, companies with established reputation and culture normally prefer graduates from school, college or university because 'it is easier to cultivate graduates as they are not influenced by any firm-based organizational culture and values yet, and they can be trained well by us' (DPE5M1).

Private companies which are in the early stages of development adopt as many talent sourcing methods as possible, many of them through personal channels such as the introduction of friends and relatives. In DPEs, referrals by friends and relatives increase the credibility of newly established companies through a sense of trust, such as 'referrals by friends and relatives are the main source of employees through networking, which add credibility to our company' (DPE7M1). It is noted that referrals by friends and relatives are also adopted in some sample SOEs. In contrast to working for newly established DPEs, jobs in SOEs are considered to be secure, which leads to severe competition among applicants. Generally, applicants have to rely on connections to seek work opportunities in SOEs; therefore, 'employees who are retiring can refer their immediate relatives to replace their positions . . . We are still preferred by employees, especially female employees, because we have better welfare systems than DPEs do' (SOE4M1).

Nevertheless, it is common for private companies at a mature stage to recruit employees through open recruitment by posting positions on the company's website and on job recruitment websites. Advertising positions on internet sites other than on the company's website is used as a method of promotion. The manager from DPE4 claimed that 'we post positions on newspapers and the internet. From our point of view, applications received via our company's website that show that applicants have not bothered to browse our website imply that they do not treat our company seriously. The possibility of their showing up for interviews and accepting a job offer is relatively low' (DPE4M1).

According to the managers' responses, employees are seldom involved in external talent sourcing, while they are widely involved in internal talent sourcing. Internal talent sourcing is part of career development and performance management, and managers 'circulate new positions among current employees before we disclose them to the public . . . as a benefit to current employees. . . . [also] recommendation from team leaders/immediate supervisors and results of performance evaluations are used as standards for identifying suitable candidates within the company' (DPE4M1). Cost efficiency is another reason to involve employees as 'we can assess the suitability of current employees for a new job based on records of their performance, observation of their supervisors and comments made by their colleagues. The information is reliable and easy to collect' (SOE3M1). Internal talent sourcing improves employee access to promotion and career opportunities, which potentially increases their commitment to the company and the possibility of staying longer.

By screening résumés and conducting job interviews, qualified employees are selected from applicants. In addition to the prior selection criteria, employers are likely to recognize the value of applicants who possess 'soft skills,' such as interpersonal or team leadership qualities, and who have the ability to reinforce the company's values at work. Fitting into the prevailing company culture has gradually become a concern of employers in the selection process.

Managers in both DPEs and SOEs address the importance of selection; however, the underlying reasons differ. In DPEs, managers are concerned to a greater extent about the associated costs: 'finding another employee implies extra cost such as advertising and organizing interviews. . . . In addition to that, investment in training also reduces a company's revenue' (DPE3M1). Recognition of a company's values and culture is another important factor that DPE organizations consider: 'our company advocates innovation. . . . An employee without creative thinking cannot fit in our company's environment, he/she leaves us eventually and our input is wasted' (DPE2M1). In SOEs, managers are more concerned about the constraints placed on them. In general, SOEs normally adopt more formal and less flexible selection standards and procedures than DPEs, making sure new recruits can fit in and perform well. Due to the nature of SOEs, managers stated: 'The majority of positions are continuing, which means we cannot lay people off easily. If we fill a job vacancy with an employee who is not suitable, the overall efficiency is affected. Although we can re-assign this employee to another position, from our experience, it is normally difficult to fit him/her in' (SOE1M1). Political, economic and social factors are a constraint which may include selection criteria such as CPC (Communist Party of China) membership: 'some selection standards used in our company are pre-set by the government body, say for instance, being a political party member' (SOE2M1).

According to managers' views, ordinary employees are rarely involved in the selection process. The reasons are quite similar to those applicable in planning – namely, employees' lack of understanding of the company's systems. Team leaders are an exception. Among the sampled companies, managers claimed that in both SOEs and DPEs, team leaders are normally involved as their opinions increase the chance of selecting suitable candidates. For example, in SOE3 the manager noted: 'Team leaders are informed about the standards and criteria in job descriptions. Compared to managers, team leaders have a better knowledge of job requirements'.

Generally speaking, staffing practices implemented in Chinese indigenous companies are closely aligned with business strategies. Skills, knowledge and personal characteristics which fit business development are first identified in the planning stage and then used as selection standards and guidelines when applicants are screened. The overall staffing process is dominated by management and facilitated by team leaders. Ordinary employees are hardly involved except in internal selection opportunities. The main reasons for the low level of employee involvement in staffing are primarily employees' lack of comprehensive understanding of business and business strategies, cost issues, impracticality and possible unfairness. At this stage of the process, the effect of these staffing practices on employees is not significant.

Training

Training is primarily related to meeting the need for skills in the organization. Nowadays, training embraces a broader aspect and forms a major part of the entire HRM system. Training helps motivate employees and ensure employees are capable of doing their jobs.

In this section, SHRM policies and practices are discussed in terms of training. The importance of issues such as strategic considerations in choosing training programs and practices used to train employees is illustrated on the basis of the managers' perspectives in the sampled companies. Detailed descriptions of links between these SHRM practices and the realization of their business goals are presented under different ownerships (i.e., SOEs and DPEs). In addition, the opportunities and level of employee involvement in the organizations are discussed in order to demonstrate whether employees are being involved in the implementation process.

In SOEs, on-the-job training is commonly provided to operational employees. The on-the-job training method takes place at work while employees are doing their actual jobs. Usually an experienced employee is assigned and serves as instructor. In managers' opinions, one of the reasons for training operational employees in such a way is cost efficiency. Normally the number of operational employees is large. Providing a large number of employees with on-the-job training maximizes return on training expenditure while production is not affected. The manager from SOE1 noted: 'Although employees who are under training at work assemble fewer qualified products than experienced employees do, we still profit from the qualified products'. On-the-job training is chosen because it is effective. It 'prepares newly-recruited employees for work as soon as possible. On-the-job training is effective in this regard as skills, techniques, and knowledge are learnt during work'. On-the-job training is common among other categories of employees such as in marketing departments, where managers noted that 'marketing skills cannot be acquired from a book. It is a combination of skills learnt from practical and accumulated real-life experiences. As a result of that, we think the best effective and efficient way is to train our marketing staff on-the-job together with experienced employees' (SOE1M1).

The off-the-job training method takes place away from normal work situations, implying that employees do not count as directly productive workers while such training takes place. In China, government bodies and policies exert more influence on SOEs than on DPEs. In this regard, SOEs enjoy less flexibility and autonomy in choosing training programs. As a result, training programs utilized in SOEs are considered to be rigid. Due to the inflexibility of selecting training programs for employees, SOEs have an alternative solution – they provide financial assistance to employees for external studies. To be specific, employees can pursue degrees after work or attend school for professional certificates. The manager from SOE2 noted: 'We can provide up to RMB15,000 to employees on the condition that they will stay with us for another five years . . . [because employees] . . . understand their needs and we can retain skilled employees. . . . [and] employees are more competitive in the job market'. However, such financial assistance is not widespread in DPEs.

Lectures are widely utilized in SOEs. Lectures have the advantage of allowing people to get away from work and concentrate more thoroughly on the training itself. This type of training is costly but sufficiently funded, and it has been proven to be effective in inculcating concepts and ideas. Expenses incurred include tuition fee for programs, accommodation, transport and meals. Managers acknowledged that lectures held by universities and professional training institutions are chosen according to the demands and strategy of the SOE and that this training minimizes the costs of having to develop training programs. Additionally, as the manager from SOE2 noted: 'After these employees are back from training, they organize lectures within our company and share what they learnt in training, which maximizes the outcome of their training'. Another manager (SOE4M1) added that as the lectures were normally too general, SOEs 'co-operate with a university which alters the general training lectures in order to reflect our business needs and required skills'.

In DPEs, on-the-job training is used to train operational employees using a similar approach to that of SOEs. With regard to off-the-job training, lectures are not as widely used in DPEs as they are in SOEs since the major concern is the cost of training regardless of the size of the company. Managers in small DPEs noted that the cost of lectures and the accompanying expenses such as 'accommodation, meals and travel' were too high (DPE7M1): 'we need to be responsible for money from our investors'. In the case of a large size private company (e.g., DPE2), managers designed and developed training programs specific to their needs and 'do not have many lectures'. DPEs face fierce competition in the open market, and timeliness of improvement in performance is of the utmost importance. Rather than focusing on using lectures which concentrate on theories and on the process of transforming theories into practices which is time-consuming, DPEs emphasize practical skills (e.g., DPE3 and DPE4).

Training programs adopted by DPEs do not show any uniform pattern. The choice of training programs is a reflection of their business strategies and characteristics. For example, companies with high tech components, such as DPE2 and DPE6, tend to design and develop their own training systems as they have resources and techniques. Companies which run massive manufacturing operations (e.g., DPE3 and DPE5) provide on-the-job training to their operational employees while outsourcing training for managerial employees. Companies that have sufficient money and resources (e.g., DPE4) normally develop their own training system, which becomes 'one of the reasons of attracting potential employees' (DPE4M1).

Training is used as a way of nurturing culture within an organization. The emphasis on company culture is frequently mentioned by managers, both in SOEs and DPEs. A general remark from one DPE illustrated that 'fitting into the culture is important to themselves [new employees] and the company' (DPE2M1), as well as strengthening the culture by 'repeated sessions . . . held every six months' (SOE2M1).

Vocational education has been undergoing reform through collaboration between industries and companies, providing a new method of training by focusing on meeting the needs of organizations. For employers, sustainable and qualified employees are available through innovative vocational schools. Some classes in these vocational schools bear the name of the companies with which the school has a cooperative relationship. In the first two years, curriculums are set up based on government requirements. In the last year, the content of curriculums is different as classes are taught using the materials provided by the company. Topics cover history, culture and skills needed for the company's operation. Students are trained to use equipment and tools that are actually used at work. In the final six months before they graduate, students work in internship/apprenticeship programs within the company. Students trained in such a way demonstrate better adaptability to working environments and higher commitment to the company. According to the manager from DPE4: 'Compared to other job applicants, their commitment to our company is potentially high; . . . . In addition, we have a stable source of skilled employees, which makes our company more competitive'.

With regard to employees' involvement and based on the views of the managers interviewed, the level of involvement of employees from SOEs and DPEs undergoing training differs among employees with different positions and educational background. Operational employees are largely involved in on-the-job training. Most of this training is essential for fulfilling job requirements. The manager from DPE3 said: 'Training provides them with minimum skills and knowledge to work on assembly lines. They are rarely involved in other training programs actively [as] the turnover rate of operative employees is high'. Employees with higher levels of education are more likely to receive training because 'employees who already have degrees are potentially competitive. In that sense, they are more actively looking for training and development opportunities' (SOE1M1).

In DPEs, employees have more autonomy and influence on training programs that are provided by the company than those working in SOEs. For example, employee training needs are relayed to HR through a supervisor, and, according to the organization's skills demand, senior management approves training. Additionally, when training programs do not fully accommodate employee needs, 'supplementary training sessions rather than amending the established training system' are provided (DPE1M1). As for SOEs, employees have less influence on training needs. SOEs face less severe competition than DPEs as they are under the regulation and support of the government. Instead, SOEs are under pressure to provide public goods and services such as transportation, building and maintaining infrastructures (i.e., telecommunication) and energy and water supplies. With the government's support, the expense of training programs is not a major concern to managers in SOEs. Due to the inflexibility of selecting employee training programs, SOEs provide financial assistance to employees to access training by themselves (e.g., SOE2). Employees are encouraged to participate in training programs outside their company and are partially or entirely reimbursed for expenses.

Training is not an isolated function; it is woven into the entire HR management system. Eligibility for training is largely based on the results of performance evaluation. In both SOEs and DPEs, managers use performance management results to identify those who are eligible for training. Employers also restrict employee eligibility on the basis of time spent with the organization: 'Due to a limited budget, we can only provide training opportunities to the people who are supposed to be valuable, with the expectation that they stay with us for a longer term' (DPE2M1). By and large training affects employees' income and is viewed as a non-monetary reward to employees. Managers 'use training as an incentive to employees and to send a signal to employees as an encouragement and reward. Also, attending such training programs may imply a possible opportunity for future promotion' (SOE3M1).

In summary, the content and methods of training vary among SOEs and DPEs. In SOEs, lectures are widely used. Training programs provided to employees in DPEs vary significantly based on business strategy, market needs, financial capability and other resources that companies apply in addressing industry competition. In addition, training programs provided to employees are different and depend on their positions in the organization. Manual workers receive basic on-the-job training aimed at basic skills. Technical employees obtain more specialized technology-oriented training, providing them with advanced knowledge and skills. Training programs can be both on-the-job and off-the-job. People with managerial responsibilities receive profession-oriented training, in particular in the areas of management and marketing, in addition to particular job-related professional training. Most of the training for managerial staff is off-the-job and is provided by management institutions and universities.

Performance management

Performance management is a process through which managers ensure employees' activities and outputs are congruent with the organization's goals. The process can be utilized to link individual employee objectives with the organization's mission and strategic plans. Additionally, it is an on-going process that ensures employees have a clear concept of how they contribute to the achievement of the overall business objective.

According to the managers who were interviewed, performance management assesses employees' performance and differs among employee groups. Firm profitability drives productivity levels required from operational/manual employees. Consequently, managers assess 'timeliness in meeting production targets and defective percentage' (DPE3M1) and review 'employees' performance regularly, making sure their performance meets our expectations' (DPE4M1). The managers in the SOEs studied share the opinions of those in the DPEs. Performance appraisals are used to measure past performance against agreed-upon productivity objectives, such as quality and quantity of goods, as well as the ability to meet deadlines. Self-assessment and peer assessment are rarely used. For administrative or professional staff, standards usually refer to absenteeism, punctuality, self-assessment, peer assessment and supervisor assessment. According to the manager from SOE4, 'Administrative and professional staff mainly provide supportive service to business operations. As a result, their performance is based on whether they can provide timely support'.

Evaluation of the performance of technicians includes administrative assessment, such as absenteeism, but also their skill level and project completeness. The manager from SOE3 said, 'We combine both objective and subjective indicators in our assessment, such as number of certificates held and supervisors' assessment'. Furthermore, the profit orientation of DPEs allows them to create and design their own performance standards. For example, managers in DPE7 are able to 'give technicians total flexibility in their job on condition that they can finish their projects. They do not have to come to work on time and they can work wherever they want' (DPE7M1). In SOEs, such a practice is impractical as usually employees are required to 'clock in and clock out' (SOE1M1).

Performance management is more than performance appraisal. Business strategy directs performance management in both DPEs and SOEs. The present study found that performance management is revised as the company develops. For example, the manager from DPE1 illustrated this development: 'We have been through different developmental stages. Initially, as a new company in the market, our strategy was to create a unique and durable product that would win as much market share as possible. During that period, we expected our employees to be proficient and creative. Our performance management, especially performance appraisals, favoured certain employees such as technicians who are highly skilled and actively involved in product development. Recently, we shifted our focus to customer satisfaction. More evaluation standards focusing on customers' feedback on the service provided by our employees have been established than before'. Performance management is also directed by business strategy in SOEs. Accordingly, when employees are expected to be team players, managers' performance appraisal on 'peer assessment about teamwork' (SOE3M1) encourages employee teamwork and employer expectations. In contrast to well-established firms that have comprehensive systems, the implementation of performance management in newly established companies is limited. For example, the manager from DPE7 said: 'The company was established around two years ago. We are understaffed and all of our employees normally multi-task. In that sense, we use general performance evaluation standards, instead of detailed and specific standards, in order to acknowledge their contributions as much as possible'.

Generally speaking, the outcomes of performance management are communicated to employees in both SOEs and DPEs, and such outcomes indicate management expectations of employees' contributions to business success. The manager from DPE4 summarized it well: 'We think individual performance matters to overall performance. . . . we consider it to be a way of showing our concern for employees. . . . Their contribution is rewarded, their drawbacks are identified, and improvement is recognized. From the results, they know what we are expecting from them and how they are performing to meet such expectations. Employees who look for development with us can make good use of the results, meet our expectations, and get promoted quickly'. Similar findings were noted in the case of managers in SOEs. Statements from SOE1M1 encapsulate performance management strategies that help employees interpret management expectations: 'When we are designing and/or revising our performance management for the coming year, we increase the level of skills and qualities required for our future development. The implications are two-fold: the first one is that employees who are already skilled to the degree we expect can be identified and advantaged; the second one is that employees are encouraged to study and fit into our developmental trend, which is to the mutual benefit of the employees and ourselves' (SOE1M1).

In both SOEs and DPEs, employees take a proactive approach to discussing the outcomes of their performance evaluation based on managers' views. The underlying reasons for this approach include: a) Outcomes of evaluation are closely related to employees' income: it is a common practice that employees' income is largely calculated on the results of their performance evaluation. The manager from DPE6 said: 'Even if we have employees who pursue career development with us, income is still vital. Nowadays, people work and expect their work to pay back. If employees are under paid for their performance, their commitment to their job and job satisfaction drops without a doubt'. b) Outcomes matter to employees' career development, as DPE2M1 claimed: 'The resources and promotion opportunities are scarce considering the number of our employees. Higher positions mean more responsibility and opportunities to get access to more resources and connections. When we need to promote an employee, we also need to justify our decision and convince other employees. We use performance management results because they are theoretically fair to everyone. It is reasonable and understandable for employees who want to develop their careers, to pay attention to the performance results.'

Although employees actively participate in discussions on the outcome of their performance evaluation, employees are rarely involved in managerial decisions regarding performance management. According to the managers' responses, the involvement of employees in SOEs and DPEs is low, and the level of involvement of employees in SOEs is even lower than that of employees in DPEs. In SOEs, the standards to be adopted in evaluation are mainly decided by the management team. The manager from SOE4 said: 'Employee representatives are invited to attend meetings with us. They collect opinions from employees about the choice of performance evaluation standards or any suggestions about current standards. Their suggestions are considered when we are making final decisions. However, the way in which senior management perceives this is different to how employees do. It is hard to tell what impact employees' suggestions can have'. Similarly, at annual meetings, employees 'can raise their concerns about any management issues' (SOE2M1), and again the impact these suggestions have on the final decisions that management makes is not known. The situation is slightly improved in DPEs as 'our employees have monthly meetings and they can communicate with their supervisors if they have any problems' (DPE3M1). However, operational/manual employees are involved at a lower level than other employees. One of the reasons that managers gave was that these 'employees are under stress to meet production targets. Unlike other employees, they are exhausted and do not have the incentive to get involved' (DPE3M1).

Besides the aforementioned lack of employee involvement, managers are also reluctant to further involve them in performance appraisals. HR managers receive 'complaints about fairness of performance evaluations . . . [which] include peer assessment and supervisors' assessment' (SOE1M1). These are subjective assessments, and yet assessments that use objective indexes 'are described as lacking in humanity'. The dilemma for supervisors and HR arises because 'employees who are close to each other talk about or share the comments from supervisors' (SOE1M1).

In summary, performance management is an indispensable component for enabling businesses to obtain competitive advantage. The criteria used in performance evaluation reflect management's expectations of business development and employee skills. Managers in both SOEs and DPEs tend to apply different performance evaluation methods to different groups of employees (i.e., operational/manual employees, administrative staff, technicians and professional staff). In addition, performance management is aligned with other SHRM practices, such as training, rewards and career development. The results of performance evaluations can be used to decide on employees' eligibility for future training, to reward employees for outstanding performance, to reward employees with preferred characteristics and relevant skills and knowledge and potentially as references for internal recruitment and career management guidelines. In terms of employee participation from the managers' perspective, employees are actively involved in discussions on the outcome of performance evaluation but are seldom involved in the managerial decision process of performance management.

Reward

From a manager's point of view, reward is a powerful tool for furthering the organization's strategic goals. First, reward has a major impact on employee attitudes and behaviours. It influences the kind of employees who remain within the organization; it can be a powerful tool for aligning current employees' interests with those of the broader organization. Second, reward is typically a significant organizational cost and thus requires close scrutiny. Third, reward is dynamic in that an organization must ensure it is comparable within a competitive labour market.

In both SOEs and DPEs, a base wage is compulsory. The composition of employees' wages varies significantly with different positions, job responsibilities, educational background and seniority.

Operational/manual employees in SOEs and DPEs are paid based on their productivity, which encompasses aspects such as quality and quantity of goods produced. This criterion is considered by managers to be fair to all employees as they are motivated by the fact that the more they produce, the more they are paid. The individual performance of operational employees affects the overall production of the organization and consequently affects profit. In this sense, after meeting pre-set targets, employees who are capable of producing extra goods receive a bonus for their efforts. As explained by one manager, operational/manual employees who exceed set production targets receive a higher pay. 'It is an incentive for them. For us, we need to save in terms of our fixed costs, such as machines' (DPE3M1). Among operational/manual employees, factors such as job responsibility, working experiences and skills level affect wages. The managers who were interviewed differentiated between employees' wages and paying extra in order 'to keep as many skilled and experienced employees as possible' (DPE1M1). The composition of wages for operational/manual employees was found to be similar across the companies studied, with only minor differences. For example, other indexes, like absenteeism rate, are included in the calculation of operational/manual employees' wages (e.g., DPE7).

Administrative/clerical employees in SOEs and DPEs provide support and service to production and are thus an 'indispensable' part of the entire system even though they are not related directly to production and profit. In order to evaluate and reward employee performance, the common practices adopted in SOEs and DPEs involve using objective indexes and rewarding employees who show outstanding performance (i.e., merit pay). The manager from DPE4 said: 'Our administrative employees are paid on the quality of support provided to other departments. Normally their wages are stable with little effect from our profit'. As for technicians and specialists (e.g., marketing and customers service), calculation of their wages is complex; it includes a number of components other than objective indexes mentioned for administrative staff. The composition of technicians' and specialists' wages is identified by managers as a reflection of business strategy. Companies other than manufacturing companies specifically address the importance of expertise as the development of the business relies on employees' skills and knowledge. For example, calculating customer satisfaction in order to enhance customer service means that 'employees who have a higher rating in their customer service can get paid more than those getting a lower rating' (SOE2M1). Similarly, firms expanding their customer base reward 'marketing specialists who visit and develop more clients' by paying them more (SOE1M1).

Besides wages, employees receive extra monetary and non-monetary rewards. In both SOEs and DPEs, employees are entitled to receive pension, unemployment insurance, medical insurance, occupational injury insurance and maternity insurance, as well as a housing allowance, under the social security system, known in Chinese as '*wuxian yijin*' (five insurances and one housing allowance). Pension, medical insurance, unemployment insurance and the housing allowance are financed by the employer and the employee. Occupational injury insurance and maternity insurance are financed by the employer alone.

Compared to employees in DPEs, rewards received by employees in SOEs tend to be work related. In other words, the rewards in SOEs are normally related to employees' work performance such as full attendance and high scoring performance evaluations. Managers believe that rewarding this performance motivates employees, but SOEs are subject to the regulations of government agencies; their use of funds and resources is less flexible than that of DPEs. In some cases, they need to justify their use of funds, which leads management to be cautious about rewarding their employees and limits the choice of rewards. Nonetheless, among the sample SOEs it is common that employers make great efforts to reward their employees beyond the scope of work. In addition, managers try to provide other benefits to their employees, 'like using the swimming pool at an employee discount, birthday vouchers, gift cards for Chinese New Year, and day care for the employees' children, . . . free lunch to all employees and free dinner if employees have to work overtime in the evening' (SOE2M1).

Employee benefits provided to employees in DPEs cover most aspects of the employees' life. In DPEs, managers face more challenges than their SOE counterparts, such as retaining skilled employees and fierce competition in the market. In contrast to SOEs, using money in DPEs is usually more flexible with fewer restrictions. If DPEs are listed on the stock exchange, share ownership options for employees could be a very efficient way of motivating and retaining them. For example, offering shares to employees with excellent performance over a number of years means that 'by holding shares, their income depends on organizational profit. They have more incentive to work and are more committed to their job and show a lower intention of leaving' (DPE1M1). Providing free accommodation and meals are commonly used incentives in DPEs. With the rise of living expenses in the cities, such as rent, groceries and transportation, free accommodation has become an important part of employee benefits. In DPE2, the manager said: 'We provide dormitories to employees for free. As we have two factory areas, we operate shuttle buses for employees to commute'. Furthermore, employees with an excellent performance record and extraordinary contributions 'can be entitled to have an apartment paid by our company' (DPE5M1).

A number of services and entertainment activities are also beneficial and available to employees in DPEs. They include free transportation between factory and town centre provided by companies (i.e., DPE1, DPE2, DPE3, DPE4 and DPE5), booking return tickets for employees going home (i.e., DPE3 and DPE5), free meals (i.e., DPE1, DPE2, DPE3, DPE4 and DPE5), free dormitory (i.e., DPE1, DPE2, DPE3, DPE4 and DPE5), day trips (i.e., DPE1, DPE2, DPE3 and DPE7) and gift vouchers for festivals (i.e., DPE1, DPE2, DPE3, DPE4, DPE5, DPE6 and DPE7). The manager from DPE2 said: 'We organize activities for employees as our dormitory is far away from the town centre. We also want single employees to meet each other as we think couples who work for us could be stable'. In DPE3, the manager said: 'To make sure our employees will be back at work after the Chinese New Year, we purchase return tickets for them'.

In both SOEs and DPEs, monetary rewards are usually given to employees based on their performance outcomes; this directly affects employees' financial income, and the competition among employees is fierce. This raises concerns of fairness, trust between peers and trust in supervisors. Managers noted that monetary rewards cause 'problems if the rewards are not given out fairly. The only option is using the outcomes of performance evaluations despite the fact that there are concerns about fairness of performance management methods and standards' (SOE1M1). Managers in DPEs share similar concerns from employees about fairness especially as 'it affects their commitment and enthusiasm towards their jobs' (DPE4M1).

Reward practices adopted and implemented in SOEs and DPEs are intended to motivate and retain employees. Generally speaking, these practices are a reflection of a business strategy which considers skills and knowledge as the source of competitive advantage to businesses. Among the sampled companies, reward is closely related to results of performance management, with high performers being eligible to receive rewards. This approach is perceived to be a relatively fair way for managers to reward their employees. In addition, employees are perceived to be involved in the reward practices. All employees are entitled to receive wages above the minimum wage level, as well as five insurances and one housing allowance. Moreover, employees are eligible for various bonus and employee benefits. With reference to whether employees are able to determine which benefits can be offered to them, the managers' responses indicate that employees are encouraged to communicate with their immediate supervisors on any issue. The immediate supervisors will pass employees' feedback to management. However, this communication is not limited to the reward system.

Career management

Career management is the combination of structured planning and the active choice of one's own professional career. As young employees in China become more educated, they are increasingly becoming aware of the expectations they have of their employment. The advantage is that people are more likely to enter an employment relationship with a clear idea of what is expected of them and what they will gain. However, a disadvantage is that if employees' expectations are not met, commitment to an organization, and therefore retention of employment, is unlikely to be sustained.

Ideally, career management includes the development of overall goals and objectives, the development of a strategy (i.e., a general means to accomplish the selected goals/objectives) and the development of the specific means (i.e., policies, rules, procedures and activities) to implement the strategy, as well as the systematic evaluation of the progress towards the achievement of the selected goals/objectives in order to modify the strategy, if necessary. Among the sampled companies, the majority of the managers remain unclear about who is responsible for career management: employees or employers. Planning and achieving employee career development individually usually involves the dedication of managers, sufficient resources and HR department capability. The managers in the sampled companies indicated that the prior factors are considered to be insufficient, especially among large companies. It is difficult for them to design and follow up every individual case. A compromise approach to career development is to provide a general guideline to employees and/or provide advice if needed, as claimed by the manager from SOE1: 'Theoretically, if career management is implemented properly, it can align employees' goals with business goals. However, in reality, it is impractical for us. Employees are supposed to know better than us about what their goals and plans for their career pathway would be. We may provide resources and help to fulfil their goals'. Conversely, where clear career pathways were provided, the manager from DPE4 asserted: 'We expect that employees are as committed to our business and development as we are. . . . If employees follow the [career] pathways, they could receive systematic training, feedback on training outcome, advice on improvement, and eventually achieve their goals. We think it is a straightforward way for employees to realize their career goal and eventually our business goal'.

Career management is an emerging concept for both managers and employees in China. Responses from managers indicate significant variations in their understanding of career management. Managers in SOEs suggest that their companies are attractive to employees because they provide career development with 'job and financial security' (SOE4M1). 'SOEs, compared to DPEs, are more secure in terms of income and positions because the majority of employees' remunerations are set by the governing body and positions are continuing. The career development of employees who follow selection criteria and get promotion is relatively stable' (SOE2M1). In contrast, in DPEs greater focus is directed at employee career needs and how employees may develop their careers with support from the organization. Managers encourage employees 'to think about what they expect at work from us and what their future will be like in our company. Also, they need to figure out how to realize their plan and what help is needed. We want employees to have a clear picture. If their expectations match ours, they tend to stay with us' (DPE1M1). Managers in both SOEs and DPEs agreed that employees are supposed to be involved in career management proactively. Managers valued employee proactivity in career management because of the positive outcomes it provided. For example, the manager from SOE2 explained: 'Employees who seek career development with us tend to sharpen their skills and look for opportunities. They are the employees who we want to retain. The others who are passive recipients are less committed to us. It is a mutual selection'. HR managers also identified difficulties in implementing career development such as the sheer numbers of employees, 'We have more than 1,000 employees. It is unrealistic for us to approach every one for career development' (SOE2M1), and because 'an individual lacks knowledge or is not fully aware of their talents and abilities. For HR managers like me, it is also difficult to identify their talents and abilities. My job is more about making career plans for employees. I think their immediate supervisors should get involved in this process, such as identifying employees' skills and talent, formulating goals, and evaluating the outcomes' (SOE2M1).

Career management is related to training and internal recruitment. In DPEs, managers combine career management with training. Managers improve employee skill levels for operational/manual employees as 'their skills affect [the organization's] overall production efficiency and consequently organizational performance' (DPE3M1). Additionally, internal recruitment assisted career management as it provided 'internal career opportunities to employees' which resulted in 'employees stay[ing] with us in pursuit of progress along the hierarchy' (SOE3M1). Furthermore, career development can be used in recruitment as a way of attracting employees. The manager from DPE2 remarked: 'Career development with us plays an important role when potential applicants are making decisions about accepting a job offer. We found applicants with a high educational background like to know how this job will be beneficial to them'.

Employee retention

Employee retention refers to the ability of an organization to retain its employees and the efforts made to retain as many capable and high performing employees as possible. In this sense, retention becomes the strategy rather than the outcome. In a business, the goal of management is usually to decrease employee turnover rate, thereby decreasing training costs, recruitment costs, and loss of talent and organizational knowledge. Nevertheless, employers can also seek to maintain only those employees whom they consider to be high performers and lay off employees whom they consider to be low performers.

Among our sampled companies, managers in SOEs encounter fewer problems in retaining employees than DPEs. The problem in SOEs is mainly related to employee redundancy instead of retention due to continuing employment contracts. Employees, especially female employees, do not want to leave the many benefits available in SOEs. As a result, managers find that because 'the structure and number of positions in SOEs is relatively fixed compared with DPEs, it is hard to establish new positions for better development' (SOE3M1). However, in recent years, labour flexibility has become more important, and job security has been gradually diminishing in SOEs (SOE3M1).

Employee retention is a more challenging issue in DPEs, especially in manufacturing companies. The managers we interviewed outlined the benefits they provide in order to reduce employee turnover. The benefits include 'the purchase of return tickets for employees who need to go home during the Chinese New Year' as well as activities that entertain employees, which can involve 'sight-seeing day trips during weekends. . . . gift-cards, accommodation. . . . As our factory is far away from the town centre, we built facilities, like supermarkets, kindergartens and gyms for employees. They can use these facilities at a lower fee' (DPE5M1). However, even these benefits may not suffice. Benefits beyond managers' control made retention unlikely: 'Employees caught up with friends from another company and then decided to leave the next day to join their friends. The reason they told us was that they wanted to work with their friends. Similar reasons include the fact that their dormitory is far from Internet Cafés, meals in the dining hall are not tasty and they are not allowed to text while working' (DPE5M1).

DPEs with well-established brands and reputations face less pressure in retaining employees, in comparison with other organizations. Companies admit that retaining employees is a complex process which involves great effort. These companies have found that 'by sharing in an ownership scheme, employees become shareholders of the company, they are motivated to work, and stay longer' (DPE1M1). In the high tech industry where the turnover rate is high, the emotional attachment that employees have to their first job encourages their return. The manager from DPE2 thought that 'most of the returning employees began their career with us and left us for specific reasons. They have told me that they came back because they wanted to work for a company where they found their first job and have a sense of emotional attachment . . . and are familiar with our working environment better than in the new workplace'. In order to retain employees, they also offer long-term contracts and monetary rewards. Other firms establish their position in the industry (e.g., they may have state-of-the-art technology in the industry), and 'employees are proud of being a member of our organization. The training and career development systems we adopt are demanding for employees. However, by going through such systems, employee growth is incredible. If our employees can see that point, they will stay with us in the long term' (DPE4M1).

Managers in DPEs all agree that younger employees (in their early 20s, the so-called 'post 80s and 90s generations') are difficult to retain. According to the manager from DPE2, 'employees who recently graduated from school . . . are active in changing jobs. They complain about stress, working environment and hours of over-time work'. Moreover, 'employees of the "post 80s and 90s" generations are normally the only child in their family. Once they complain to their parents about how stressful the job is and how little they make, their parents tell them to quit right away' (DPE6M1).

Managers in the sampled companies identified a series of practices and policies used to retain employees, financially and emotionally. Most of them agreed that employee retention does not involve an isolated set of practices. To retain employees, practices from other HR functions are combined, such as training, rewarding, career development and internal recruitment. For example, the manager from DPE2 said: 'Training can be considered to be a way we retain our skilled employees because our training program is tailored to our employees. Skills and knowledge learnt can be used in their daily job directly, which is very efficient and convenient for employees'. The manager from DPE4 said: 'If employees can see their bright career future with us, it is easy for us to retain them'.

So far, the discussion in this chapter has been based on interviews with managers. The following section will focus on the results of interviews with employees in order to gain a more comprehensive understanding of the adoption of SHRM/HPWS and the impact on employees in these Chinese enterprises.

Employees' responses

The literature review in chapter 2 indicated that employees can form perceptions about management's intentions and attitudes towards them by interpreting HR practices and policies enacted by the organization (Whitener, 2001). Employees put into practice the HPWS implemented by management and are critical in the process. The manner in which employees interpret HR practices affects their attitudes and behaviours and eventually the outcome. In this research, employees were interviewed on their opinions about HPWS and the effects of the practices on these employees, in correspondence with the interview questions posed to the managers in the same organizations. This method allowed cross-checking of responses in order to identify similarities and differences between managers' and employees' perspectives of HR policies and practices.

Staffing

Staffing is considered to be the first HR function that employees experience in a company. Responses from the managers interviewed indicate that staffing generates a large number of job applicants, which ensures that vacancies are filled by qualified applicants. Managers in the sampled companies implement appropriate staffing practices to identify skills, knowledge and personal characteristics which align with business strategies. From the managers' perspective, staffing is a process dominated by management and facilitated by team leaders. Ordinary employees are hardly involved except in internal selection opportunities.

This section elaborates on employees' awareness of staffing practices and the effects on their attitudes and behaviours. In comparison with managers in general, and HR managers in particular, who are actively involved in the entire process of staffing, the employees interviewed indicated low levels of participation, reflecting the findings from managers' responses about the involvement of employees in this regard.

Employees in both SOEs and DPEs indicated that they had their own way of interpreting job descriptions and specifications as signals sent from management. Some employees used these signals as an informal way of discovering the company's developmental direction and future strategic focus. For example, SOE2E1 said: 'Job descriptions of new jobs specify the qualifications and requirements needed. These specifications tell me the direction in which this company is heading'. DPE2E2 also was able to interpret the organization's developmental direction by claiming the company was 'recruiting senior managers for customer services which implies that the company would expand its customer base, instead of lowering production cost'. Paying attention to job descriptions and specifications helped employees (e.g., SOE2E1 and DPE6E2) understand the signals their organizations were sending for long-term development.

The majority of employees in SOEs interviewed indicated their awareness of recruitment procedures. The level of awareness differed according to their positions. Professional staff and technicians (e.g., SOE1E1, SOE2E2 and SOE4E2) showed a relatively high level of awareness; they could obtain recruitment information from multiple sources via internet, career expos and other similar avenues. Specifically, SOE1E1 was recruited as a graduate following an on-campus career event. He said: 'Recruitment is targeted towards recent graduates. I searched for the information about this company via the internet. A career exhibition is held regularly on campus. HR specialists answer any questions and explain the recruitment procedures on the spot. Besides, the selection criteria are listed explicitly on the company's website'.

In contrast to professional staff and technicians, operational and clerical staff in SOEs showed a relatively low level of awareness. Normally, they perceived their work as requiring no specific skills/knowledge, as was the case of SOE2E1, an operational employee who works on an assembly line with no supervisory responsibility. He said: 'I was recruited when I graduated from vocational school. I am not quite clear about what the requirements are. Basically, in my mind, this position does not require particular skills'. The same situation was experienced by SOE3E2, an administrative staff who commented that 'my job does not require very specific skills. . . . I went through the interviews without any preparation'. It is not unusual for employees to learn about the interview procedures at the interviews themselves; SOE4E1 said: 'I was not informed about the recruitment procedures until I went through it myself'. Nevertheless, employees who care about the future of their careers appear to concern themselves with recruitment procedures. For instance, SOE4E2 checked online forums, and SOE3E3 said: 'I contacted my friend who had been with this company and asked him for details about their recruitment procedures and selection criteria'.

The interviewees indicated that recruitment information is usually accessible only to existing employees, while remaining unclear to potential employees. After employees are recruited in SOEs, they are informed about internal recruitment opportunities by the HR specialist and on the intranet. SOE1E2 had been with the same company for more than three years, and he described the internal recruitment process he had experienced when the company restructured: 'Employees like myself were informed by the HR department about the availability of new positions. I was allowed to choose the positions I preferred and the suggestions of my supervisor were considered in the final decision'. However, employees indicated different levels of accessibility of information between job applicants and existing employees, such as SOE1E3, who said: 'Applicants are not as informed as I am'.

Team leaders demonstrated a higher level of awareness of recruitment standards than ordinary employees, consistent with the responses received from managers. For example, SOE3E1, a technician who has been in the organization for seven years, believed that 'as I am a team leader, I am involved in first-round interviews occasionally, which makes me know more about recruitment'. Uncommon circumstances also enable positions in SOEs even though recruitment practice is unclear. SOE4E1 said: 'I got in because I took the position which my aunt used to hold. It was common practice five years ago and has become rare recently'. Another case is SOE2E4, an accountant who had been with the company for only six months. She knew where to find information on recruitment; however, as she had already been given the job, she did not have to access this information.

In DPEs, potential employees obtain recruitment information in various ways, such as via the internet (E2DPE1), newspapers (E2DPE4) and job agencies (E3DPE1). In the case of operational/manual employees in DPEs, especially those in manufacturing, the number of employees to be recruited is large. Posters are an efficient way of recruiting these employees (e.g., E1DPE3, E2DPE3 and E3DPE3).

In DPEs, employees who have high educational backgrounds proactively seek information about the recruitment process, while other employees are simply recipients of such a process. For example, employees of E1DPE2 and E2DPE2 were recruited as graduates from university. Both were familiar with the recruitment procedures, as this information could be found on the internet, and they attended a career exhibition on campus. Both thought the competition was fierce. They prepared for interviews based on experiences shared online. In contrast, DPE3E4, a high school drop-out, looked for a job which did not require much education. He did not have to prepare for an interview. He said: 'I saw the poster and I was interviewed immediately. They asked me some general questions such as age, marital status, and experience on assembly lines'. The views expressed by employees in DPEs indicate that recruitment methods usually evolve as the business develops. In the early stage of development, employees are usually referred to the company by acquaintances, friends and relatives. DPE1E1 said: 'I joined this company around the time it was founded. Ten years back, there was not much policy and practice in place. I was referred by my friend. Currently, we do have a comprehensive system which has been revised to catch up with the changes. I have been informed about the changes'. Another example is DPE7, a newly established company with around 50 employees. Current employees were not aware of its recruitment practices. DPE7E1 said: 'I was referred by my relative. I am afraid we do not have formal recruitment procedures. The most efficient way for us to obtain any HR information is by talking to the company's HR staff. In addition to that, any updates are circulated via emails'.

As mentioned earlier, managers' interviews indicate that co-operation between vocational schools and businesses provides companies with sustainable and stable sources of skilled employees. Employees who are recruited in this way are informed about the process through their schools. DPE2E3 is an operational employee who was recruited through a vocational school. He said: 'I was allocated to this company because of the partnership my school has with this company. I worked here for six months as an apprentice before I graduated. My supervisors assessed my work performance in the past six months and offered me this job'. Likewise, in DPE4, operational/manual employees are recruited from the vocational schools with which this company has long-term training programs. According to the company, the employees are selected upon passing the school examinations. Basically no recruitment practices are involved at this stage. After the employees have been with the company for more than one year, they are provided with opportunities to be promoted. They are well informed on the criteria and selection procedures. Experienced employees are in great demand; therefore, being aware of or understanding the recruitment process does not concern them. DPE2E4 and DPE2E5 were recruited as experienced applicants. Since experienced marketing specialists are in short supply, they were confident of finding jobs.

In terms of participation, it was found that employees in both SOEs and DPEs are involved to the same extent in recruitment and selection at specific levels. As recruitment is a process occurring before potential employees officially join companies, most of the employees do not consider that they are involved either before or after joining the companies.

As for the existing employees in SOEs, they are reluctant to participate in recruitment and selection activities and to raise their concerns about their participation. Ordinary employees are invited to attend employee meetings where they can express their concerns on any issues, including recruitment and selection. For example, SOE1E1 said: 'A job analysis is undertaken by the HR department and is submitted to senior management for approval. In most cases, we simply follow the recruitment policy and procedures rather than ask questions'. Fairness of selection procedures is questioned frequently, rather than the criteria themselves. SOE2E2 claimed: 'A meeting attended by all employees is held annually. It is difficult for us to have a say in that meeting. I am worried about fairness of recruitment, especially selection, which affects my payment significantly'.

In the case of employees who have supervisory responsibility (i.e., team leader), the opinions of these employees affect the decision of recruitment and selection.

Final decisions are still made by senior managers, as SOE3E1 claimed: 'I am involved in the process of recruitment and selection. The potential employees who may be assigned to my team are interviewed by me and approved by senior managers'. Employees are also concerned about trust at the workplace, as noted by SOE4E3: 'I am not sure whether my suggestions will be followed up and I am not sure whether it will jeopardize my future interest at work'.

Entry-level employees and operational employees consider themselves not to be extensively involved in the recruitment process. For example, DPE3E1, DPE3E2, DPE3E3 and DPE3E4 did not think that they were involved in recruitment practices, as they were entry-level employees. They were stressed at work due to the very fast pace required and therefore did not show any interest in participating in recruitment processes.

From the perspective of employees in SOEs, staffing practices affect employee attitudes and behaviours moderately. Employees in the sampled companies frequently mentioned trust between colleagues and supervisors during the entire process of recruitment and selection. In contrast to Western culture, connection or relationship (*guanxi*) plays an important role in China. SOE1E3 indicated: 'I do know that some of my colleagues got in through referrals by senior managers. They might be qualified for their jobs, but I still think it is unfair to others, especially to those who do not have strong connections with the management team'. Feelings of mistrust were evident as SOE3E3 said: 'I was sometimes de-motivated reading internal recruitment information. I am not sure whether it is "customized" for someone in particular'. SOE1E2 shared a similar comment: 'The transparency of recruitment and selection has significantly increased recently, however I still feel uncomfortable occasionally. I am quite concerned that my effort at work is not recognized, which definitely affects my motivation at work'.

Overall, employees from SOEs and DPEs were found to be aware of recruitment practices and policies implemented in their organizations. The level of their awareness varies depending on the different positions, educational background and expectations of their current jobs. Normally, employees with knowledge-oriented positions, higher educational background and high expectations show a relatively high level of awareness. Consequently, they are actively involved in recruitment practices, especially in internal recruitment. Employees with supervisory responsibility are involved more extensively, compared with ordinary employees; these employees interview potential applicants and may affect managerial decisions. With regard to perceptions of recruitment practices and policies, employees are concerned about fairness and show a low level of trust in the workplace. As for employee participation, employees show hesitation and a low level of participation in this area, which reflects the findings seen in managers' responses.

Training

Training helps motivate employees and ensure employees are capable of performing their jobs. Managers' interviews highlighted important issues, such as strategic considerations in training programs and methods selected to train employees.

Training is implemented to ensure that employees obtain the required skills and apply these skills at work in order to enhance individual and organizational performance.

In SOEs, mentoring is widely utilized as an on-the-job employee training method. Employees (e.g., SOE1E1 and SOE1E3) described mentoring as a process of training whereby employees work closely with their mentors in teams. Derived from one-on-one training programs, employees are of the opinion that a relatively 'loose' on-the-job training is adopted. Employees (e.g., SOE1E2 and SOE2E1) are trained by reading work manuals, and they can approach senior or experienced colleagues for assistance.

Similar to the responses of managers in SOEs, employees indicated that training programs after work and reimbursement of the costs encourages employees to enhance their skills and knowledge. Employees SOE2E2 and SOE2E4 said: 'We are encouraged to pursue a high goal and we receive monetary support from the company. We are going to sit the CPA examination this year. The company covers nearly half of the cost'. Additionally, SOE3E1 stated: 'We have a number of training programs, such as outsourcing and job rotation. We can also attend school and the cost is covered partially by the company'. E2SOE4 confirmed: 'I am fully aware of the training programs and practices. I think the company's re-imbursement of part of the training program attended by employees in their after-work hours is helpful to the employees' career'.

Employees in DPEs also pointed out that on-the-job training is being widely used in their companies. Training is conducted in a few forms: short-term and long-term training programs as well as online training. DPE1E1 said: 'We are trained through short-term training programs, usually only taking two hours. The program covers the new systems or techniques introduced, or any improvement made on products'. Training can also be longer term over, for instance, two months (DPE7E1), or may take the form of consultations with senior staff (DPE3E1 and DPE3E2) and group meetings (DPE2E4). Online training is also offered; for example, DPE2E3 described the E-learning system adopted in their organization: 'It is designed by knowledgeable professional staff . . . This system is exclusive and only current employees can get access to it. It is updated and cutting-edge . . . [and] . . . contains techniques and theory which becomes part of the employee performance management system'.

The training programs run in DPEs give employees opportunities to obtain professional certificates. DPE4E1 stated: 'I know the training programs are linked together in a complex way. Every time there is an introduction of a new module, new operating system, new techniques, we are required to attend training sessions. In parallel, we have another training certificate system; we need to study and pass the tests to get the certificates at beginner, intermediary and advanced levels. They are recognized nationally'. There is also another internal training and certification system which applies to the current organization and is not recognized by other companies. For example, DPE6E2 claimed: 'The level of certificate we obtain affects the position and payment per assignment. However, if we leave this company, the certificate expires after three months'.

Similarly to SOEs, training programs in DPEs are exclusive according to seniority, as described by DPE2E2: 'I am new to this organization. I know that after working here for more than two years I am eligible to be sent to advance training programs. The company organizes several training programs every year. Some are held by senior and experienced employees, some are outsourced'. Additionally, in DPEs, employees are encouraged to study after work. Employees from DPE5 (E1, E2 and E3) agreed: 'The training we attend is on-the-job training. We are encouraged to pursue higher levels. We can sign up for distance training programs which post our learning materials monthly. These are certified by the company and the company covers half of the cost'. Not all the employees in the sample DPEs are aware of and participate in training programs. Some experienced employees (e.g., DPE7E3 and DPE6E3) rarely attend training programs and do not perceive training as being necessary for them.

The majority of employees in SOEs (e.g., SOE1 and SOE2) think they are passive recipients of training practices. According to managers, employees are encouraged to participate; however, employees are not proactively involved. SOE1E1 shared a similar opinion: 'On-the-job training is very helpful to me. Everything I learnt is practical. The training policy is set by management. I followed the regulation and policy as a passive recipient'.

In the case of employees who are involved in training programs, little evidence shows that employees participate in managerial decisions on training programs. Employees in SOE4 (E1, E2 and E3) agreed that they were involved in training programs held by the company at different times; however, there was no evidence that they were involved in the managerial decision process of choosing the training practices to be implemented. SOE3E3 said: 'I was sent to another location for training the year before. But I am not involved in making decisions about what training practices are to be implemented'.

Employees in some of the sample DPEs (e.g., DPE1, DPE2 and DPE4) actively communicate with their supervisors and make suggestions for managerial decisions in choosing training programs. The employees' responses indicate that they prefer to communicate directly with their immediate supervisors. The methods of communication include talking, regular group meetings, text messages or emails, bulletin boards and suggestion boxes. For example, DPE4E3 said: 'We can communicate with managers. The most efficient way is weekly meetings. Questions are followed up in time and we get feedback in the next weekly meeting'. Employees in DPE1 (E1, E2, E3, E4 and E5) stated that they were involved in training programs. DPE1E3 noted: 'We can nominate training programs to our supervisors or HR staff'. Other employees in the sample DPEs realized that they were encouraged to voice their suggestions, but were concerned about confidentiality and any adverse consequences. For example, DPE3 is a manufacturing company where operational/manual employees make up a large percentage of the total number of employees. The most efficient way for them to communicate with management is to send text messages and call their immediate supervisors (DPE3E1 and DPE3E3). However, the confidentiality and usefulness of their messages is a concern to them. They also question the applicability of making suggestions. In DPE6, employees (DPE6E2 and DPE6E3) were of the view that although they did have time to attend training and talk to supervisors, they worried about the impact of their input on decisions made by management. Moreover, the availability of training programs posed limits on employees' participation in training programs. For example, DPE5E3 said: 'The training offered to managerial people should be much more than what have been offered to us. The way we can raise our concerns is by talking to our supervisors'.

In general, the majority of employees feel unsure about whether they can affect managerial decisions in training programs. Some employees (i.e., DPE7E2 and DPE7E3) were also concerned about the suitability of training programs, since they felt that it was impossible for general training programs to satisfy everyone's needs.

In both SOEs and DPEs, training programs are welcomed by employees, and they influence employees' attitudes positively. Firstly, training is viewed as an investment by employers and interpreted by employees favourably. Training could play a role in retaining employees, as SOE1E3 said: 'It would be good if more training programs are provided. Training is expensive. It is perceived to be an investment by the company which is a positive signal to me. The more I learn, the more value is created. If I get paid more, I will stay'. SOE2E4 agreed: 'If I could get my CPA while I am working here, I think I would stay and follow my career development'. Second, some employees (SOE3E1, SOE3E2 and SOE3E3) believed training could be considered to be another kind of reward scheme because only those with outstanding performance can be selected to attend training programs. In addition, training, qualifications or skills obtained are seen by the employees as being beneficial for future career development. Third, employees can make good use of training programs to improve their skill sets and networks. For example, SOE2E2 said: 'Training is very important to me. I want to make good use of the resources this company has. As money is not an issue to our SOE, it would be good if I could have access to more training programs. If attending training programs is counted as part of my workload, it will be even better'. SOE4E3 also reflected: 'By attending a training program held in another city, I get to know a number of new colleagues. . . . Training is more than studying; it means a lot, new connection, new culture, and new way of thinking and so on'.

Employees in DPEs perceived training as being beneficial to their work. In DPE1, employee DPE1E1 said: 'I think the comprehensive training programs help me learn while working here. . . . Training provides familiarity and helps me adapt to my job, as well as increasing my connections to people which will be helpful if I am seeking another job . . . and . . . beneficial to my future.' Training also encourages positive attitudes claimed by DPE2E1: 'Training facilitates my development. If my development is smooth, I do not see any reasons for me to leave'. DPE4E1 also claimed to feel 'very proud of being involved in the training programs in our company, as the company is recognized nationally and known for its quality'.

Unlike employees in the aforementioned companies, employees in DPE3 and DPE5 believed that their jobs were interchangeable; in other words, if they quit, their jobs would be filled quickly by others. Training only enabled them to work in the company, but they did not obtain many useful skills for their future. These employees remained in the company if their income was satisfactory.

In summary, training programs are perceived by employees in SOEs and DPEs to affect their commitment positively and reduce their intention of leaving. In some companies, the robustness and recognition of training within their industry enhance employees' sense of pride. Training can be interpreted by employees to be recognition from management. In comparison with responses received from the managers studied, employees in SOEs indicated the extensive availability of lectures and on-the-job training and were aware of mentoring initiatives. In DPEs, training is carried out in more varied and flexible forms than in SOEs, such as online training, which is more customized to fulfil specific requirements and fit into companies' future development. The fact that employees are becoming educated and focused on their own development within an organization means that the importance of training is being emphasized by employees. These employees attend training not only for development in their current jobs but also for their future career development. With regard to employees' participation, employees are generally involved in training and rarely in managerial decisions on training. They are entitled to make suggestions; however, most prefer to be passive recipients of training practices and policies, taking trust issues into account. The next section will shift the focus to performance management.

Performance management

Performance management is adopted by management to ensure employees' activities and output are consistent with the organizations' goals. From managers' perspectives, performance management is mainly utilized to assess employees' past performance; it links individual employees' objectives with the organization's mission and strategic plan. Performance management is also closely related with other HR functions in the same organization. However, it is not clear whether the same views are shared by employees. Therefore, a number of issues are discussed here: whether employees are aware of performance management being implemented, whether employees participate in such practices and how these policies and practices affect employees' attitudes and behaviours.

Most of the employees in the SOEs studied showed a high level of awareness of performance standards and criteria adopted in their organization. Standards of performance were evident for SOE1E1, who believed that 'the result of my performance evaluation closely relates to my wage. I was assessed on how many customers I visited, how many customers I maintained and how many new customers I developed'. An awareness of other standards of performance was indicated by SOE1E2, who claimed: 'My performance is evaluated based on my punctuality. My performance evaluation reports consist of self-assessment and supervisor assessment', and by SOE1E3, who said: 'My performance is mainly evaluated on the basis of a project, not individual performance'. Yet others are informed of performance standards through a performance index sheet (e.g., SOE2E1, SOE3E2 and SOE3E3).

Awareness of performance standards also highlights where inconsistency exists between performance and employee wage. Inconsistencies are evident in SOEs where constraints are set by external controls. For example, SOE2E2 commented: 'My wage does not vary according to my performance. My performance is evaluated quarterly which affects only my promotion'. SOE2E3 also admitted that 'wage is fixed and it is set based on how many years and what administrative level I am on'.

In DPEs, performance management systems include more components than those in SOEs, a view shared by the managers studied in the sample organizations. Most of the employees in DPEs are well informed on how performance is evaluated. DPE1E2 illustrated that 'the performance management system is composed of self-assessment, peer-assessment and supervisor-assessment. We receive a performance evaluation form monthly and annually, depending on the type of position. Operational staff is evaluated monthly and others on an annual basis'. DPE1E3 described very similar performance management systems and added that 'the employees who rank last three will be reassigned to another job or demoted'.

Different criteria apply for different positions and industries. Among operational employees, performance is normally assessed on the quantity of products with variation depending on their tenure and skill levels. DPE5E1 agreed that 'the positions of operative staff have three levels, and the assessment standards are applied differently'. Timeliness and percentage of failure are counted as components of their performance evaluation (e.g., DPE3E1, DPE3E2, DPE4E1, DPE4E2, DPE5E1 and DPE5E2).

In the case of clerical staff and specialists (e.g., marketing, customer service and HR), performance is assessed by combining objective and subjective indexes. In DPE4, the marketing specialist (DPE4E5) said, 'My performance is evaluated based on the satisfaction of my customers'. Customer evaluation of service includes assessing the specialists' performance and affects their wage and/or bonus (e.g., DPE6E1, DPE6E2 and DPE6E3). For administrative employees, the performance management systems consist of components such as self-assessment, peer assessment, supervisor assessment, workload and other objective indexes (e.g., absenteeism). The combination and percentage of these components varies in different companies. In DPE7, employees were largely assessed by objective indexes, while in DPE1, employees (E1 and E3) were evaluated by subjective assessment methods.

In terms of employee participation in performance management in SOEs, employees (e.g., SOE1 and SOE3) were interviewed on the results of their performance assessment. Employee SOE1E1 stated: 'The criteria of performance evaluations are circulated and we are informed about any changes. We are allowed to make suggestions or talk to our supervisors if we have any questions. I am quite satisfied at the moment and I may approach my supervisors if any further changes are not clear'. According to the responses received, employees indicated that their suggestions and questions were followed up promptly (e.g., SOE3E1 and SOE3E2). In other SOEs (e.g., SOE2), wages were mainly fixed with variation of pay determined by the impact of sick leave and absenteeism rate. The employees felt that they were rarely involved or had a say in performance management and that this aspect was the responsibility of HR, as SOE4E3 said: 'I do not want to get involved because it is too bureaucratic for me. The underlying connections and relationships are too complicated. I am not sure what the consequences will be if I am involved. I want to focus on my job'.

The interviews also show that employees are concerned about the fairness of setting standards but are less comfortable in voicing their opinions. SOE3E3 noted: 'We discuss performance management issues during weekly group meetings. I do think the standards favour particular groups of people. However, I would not like to say something that causes unnecessary trouble'. Similarly, SOE1E3 said: 'I do not think all assessment adopted is fair but it is a big company. I guess it is extremely difficult to be fair'. SOE4E1 felt vulnerable when expressing opinions publicly and indicated that employees preferred to communicate with their supervisors in private.

In contrast, the responses from employees in DPEs indicate that the level of involvement of these employees in performance management is high. In DPE1, all employees who were interviewed felt that they were involved in the process as they were allowed to assess their colleagues' performance. They were also informed of the results of the performance evaluation and could discuss any issues or problems with their supervisors. Employees from DPE2 also believed that they were involved in the performance management process. Electronic systems had enhanced the flexibility and efficiency of communication. For example, DPE2E4 said: 'SMS via mobile phone is popular. Any questions can be sent to our supervisors and managers. We can even talk to HR staff and my supervisors about some private problems encountered. Unlike other office workers, I cannot sit in front of my desk. With SMS I am updated and informed'.

Managers in DPEs are perceived to be open to comment and communicate with employees. In DPE2, employees thought their management was very open to comments about policies implemented. However, they were not sure whether they could influence the final decision. In DPE3, the mobile numbers of managers were available to all employees. Employees could text and call their managers whenever they were not satisfied, as well as ask questions beyond the sphere of their jobs.

Group discussions and communications with immediate supervisors are perceived to be efficient in solving problems in performance management. DPE4E3 stated that 'talking to supervisors is efficient. So are group meetings. We have a suggestion box but we do not use it'.

Although employees in DPEs are encouraged to make suggestions about performance management policies, they are not sure about whether their opinions will influence final decisions. In DPE1, all employees agreed that performance evaluation was related to rewards such as bonuses, extra days of paid leave, promotion and training opportunities. However, they did not think that their opinions about performance management policies would be adopted. To be specific, DPE6E1 said: 'The existing performance system is designed by our headquarters.

It seems impossible for an individual employee like myself to have an impact on it. It never occurs to me that I can make suggestions about it'. Additionally, DPE5E1 noted: 'I do not think we can have a say on performance management because we are entry level employees. Even if I have an opinion, I am afraid it is a waste of my time to talk to anyone'. Other DPE employees felt the use of suggestions boxes was 'very old fashioned and unprotected' (e.g., DPE7E3). Therefore, making suggestions on performance management policy was impractical. One comment received indicated that although performance assessment was 'too rigid . . . they could not figure out a better way of doing it' (DPE7E1).

In SOEs, it is widely accepted that becoming involved in and informed about performance management increases employees' motivation. First, results of performance management affect employees' income. Employees SOE3E1, SOE3E2 and SOE3E3 agreed that performance management was critical to them because the results of performance affect their work in terms of promotion and wages. If their performance can be assessed as fairly as possible, their job satisfaction is assumed to be increased. Second, being informed by managers is interpreted by employees as confirmation that they are members of the company. Employees SOE1E1 and SOE1E3 admitted that 'knowing more details about policies and practices implemented helps us be clear on how to work efficiently'. SOE4E1 said: 'Knowing how our performance is assessed makes me feel that procedures are transparent and fair. If I can be involved, I will know more about how it works. It has a positive impact on my job satisfaction because I have a feeling of belonging'. Third, standards used in performance management inform employees about the qualifications needed at work. SOE4E2 said: 'I think knowing more details about how our performance is evaluated is beneficial to my job. If my performance is recognized by the company, I will have more motivation'.

The effects of performance management on employees' attitudes and behaviours identified by employees in DPEs are similar to those in SOEs. Employees were motivated because of their excellence in their current job (DPE1E2), the strong connection between performance and rewards (DPE1E3), the company's demand for skills and performance (DPE4E4) and the low intention of leaving (DPE2E2).

Apart from these positive responses, some employees are de-motivated by current performance management systems. Among the SOE employees interviewed, SOE2E2 said: 'Our wages are not calculated based on our performance, which means it is not necessary to work hard. If I have to work with people holding such an opinion or our project involves these kinds of people, the progress of my work is slowed'. SOE3E1 indicated: 'Performance management directs me with regard to the qualifications, skills and characteristics needed for the job. It motivates me'. SOE2E3 noted: 'Most of my colleagues hold continuing positions. The results of performance management do not affect their job security unless under extreme circumstances. It is unfair to those who are on fixed-term contracts and are new to this company. The workload is heavy for them'. Among the DPE employees interviewed, DPE6E1 worried about whether his efforts were recognized if his performance was largely decided by customer feedback. Other concerns included a trade-off between time-consuming and comprehensive assessment (DPE4E1).

In summary, performance management constitutes a significant element for employees as it is closely related to their wages and consequently affects their quality of life. In both SOEs and DPEs, employees are generally well aware of performance management policies. Compared to employees in SOEs, those in DPEs believed their managers were more open to communication and showed more flexibility in implementation of policies. Given the major effects of performance management results, employees expressed their concerns about the fairness of the criteria set. In terms of employee participation in performance management, employees are active in communicating with their supervisors through meetings and by sending emails/text messages. Most employees indicated that being aware and participating in the performance management process increased employees' commitment and reduced their intention to leave. A few employees felt that it took too much time to participate and were de-motivated in this regard. The following section will further illustrate the rewards system and its influence on employees.

Rewards

Rewards are very important for both managers and employees. For managers, a number of reward practices are in place to motivate them and enhance organizational performance. For employees, rewards can be monetary and non-monetary; they affect employees' well-being and commitment directly.

In SOEs, most employees are aware of the composition of their income. The common practice in SOEs is to set the base wage according to an employee's position. SOE1E1, a marketing specialist, said: 'It is a rule that my payment includes base wage and extra is calculated based on project profit'. His opinion was shared by employees from other SOEs (e.g., SOE1E3, SOE2E2 and SOE3E3). Deductions are made in order to discourage employees from being late and having low work efficiency. SOE1E2 said: 'My wage was fixed and agreed when I was offered this job. It may be deducted if I disobey the company's policies'.

Besides remuneration, employees receive additional benefits, either in a monetary or non-monetary form. SOE3E1 said: 'We receive gifts for New Year, birthdays and other Chinese traditional festivals. Female employees can have half day off when it is International Women's Day. If both of the couples are working for the same company, one of them can go off earlier to pick up their kids'. Another employee, SOE3E2, said: 'My colleagues who are not local residents can leave the company one to three days in advance to travel to their hometown, avoiding peak time traffic'. Other benefits described by employees include an extra two weeks' maternity and parental leave (e.g., SOE3E1 and SOE3E2), day trips (e.g., SOE4E2 and SOE4E3) and extra paid leave for outstanding performance (e.g., SOE2E2 and SOE4E3). According to the feedback from employees, reward practices in SOEs are less flexible than in DPEs, as explained by SOE2E3: 'In SOEs, we do not have as much flexibility as a private company has. In other words, the monetary rewards we receive are much less. If my performance is assessed as outstanding in three consecutive evaluations, it will be advantageous to my promotion'.

The composition of remuneration in DPEs adapts to changes in circumstances more quickly than in SOEs. Most of the employees were aware of how these circumstances affected the way their wages were calculated. DPE1E2 said: 'We have formulas for wage calculation. The feedback from our customers is part of my assessment. If the rate of my customers' satisfaction is in the top 5 percent among all marketing staff, I receive a bonus . . . if for the coming quarter, our target is to expand our customer base, the bonus will be increased for marketing specialists'.

Employees in DPEs are rewarded in extensive ways, including accommodation, transportation and meals. DPE2E2 said: 'Dinner is provided for employees who have to work overtime. Pay rate doubles if weekly working hours exceed 40'. Entertainment is organized such as dinners for New Year, Chinese New Year, day trips and matches (DPE1E3). Providing free dormitories for employees is welcomed among employees (DPE2E3 and DPE2E4). Furthermore, DPE1E1 noted: 'Employees who show excellent performance for more than five years or make an extraordinary contribution to the company, can purchase an apartment at cost which the company has built'. This scheme significantly lowers employees' living expense. Facilities in the vicinity of the factory such as hotels, supermarkets and restaurants increase employee satisfaction (DPE5E2). Shuttle buses are operated weekly, saving time for employees (DPE3E1).

In terms of employee participation in performance management, employees' willingness to be involved varies. The interviews indicate that employees in the sampled SOEs (SOE1 and SOE4) showed their willingness to be involved in decision-making with regard to the rewards system. For example, SOE4E3 said: 'If possible, I want to get involved in designing the reward policies. The policies adopted favour some parties in this organization in my view. I want to make sure I am not disadvantaged'. In other sampled SOEs, employee perceptions are that it is impractical for them to become involved. SOE3E1 claimed: 'It is because a SOE is mostly regulated by governments. I am afraid management does not have much autonomy to offer us rewards even if they wish to. I guess individual employees have even less effect on these policies'. SOE2A1 said: 'Managers are slow to respond'. Other SOE3 employees were concerned about the fairness of the reward system. To be specific, SOE3E1 thought reward policies might favour a particular group of employees in the organization and that becoming involved was risky.

The level of DPE employee involvement is higher than in SOEs. All the interviewed employees from DPE1 believed they were involved in the reward policies with due consideration to equality and fairness. In particular, DPE1E1 believed that the company was generous in rewarding employees. Similar feedback was received in DPE2. DPE2E1 commented: 'We have SMS and online systems to communicate with supervisors/managers about any issues concerned'. Employees in DPE2 believed that they benefitted from the employee reward system, as free accommodation, food and transportation are available to all employees regardless of how many years they have been with their current employer and regardless of their status within the organization. Since they are satisfied, they are motivated to participate in the managerial process of making or affecting decisions.

However, entry-level employees in major manufacturing companies are rarely involved and seldom affect managerial decisions. For example, DPE3E1 said: 'Employees like us are not involved at all. We can communicate with our supervisors. Some of our personal concerns and questions are noted and solved. I doubt that I have an effect on managerial decisions'.

Monetary rewards are important to employee motivation in SOEs. For example, SOE1E1 said: 'Honestly, monetary rewards are my motivation to work hard. The more I worked, the more I earned'. Some employees also value non-monetary rewards. SOE2E2 commented: 'It is hard to deny that monetary rewards are important, but sometimes, non-monetary rewards matter to me'. SOE3E1 agreed: 'I do hope more rewards can be put into effect. Rewards motivate me, both monetary and non-monetary. They are the recognition from employers'. Opportunities to have a say in managerial decisions motivate employees. For example, SOE4E3 said: 'If I can get involved, I think I will be motivated to work harder, knowing my efforts are recognized and I am treated fairly. At the workplace, the relationship is beyond what it looks like, more complicated than I expected. I want to be rewarded for every contribution I make, even if it might be too unrealistic'.

Employees from the sample DPEs also appreciate non-monetary rewards, which create a feeling of belonging and accomplishment. Employees (e.g., DPE2E1) from DPE2 said: 'Working overtime is very stressful. By providing food and drinks, extra pay for extra hours, I have more motivation. After long hours' working, we sacrifice our time with family and friends; food comforts us at a certain level. Imagine if we had to cook after a long day, it would make our life miserable'. DPE3E3 explained that 'even if we have to share rooms with others, it is not a big issue in comparison with paying a big proportion of our salary in rent. The accommodation is close to the office and we save on transport costs. I see it as an invisible income for me'. DPE4E1 thought the rewards were more than monetary; the skills learnt are part of the rewards.

In general, SOEs have less choice in rewarding their employees. The common practice is a bonus based on project profit, supplementary payments for festivals, free working meals and transport. In DPEs, employees are rewarded with more generous and flexible offers. They can access share ownership and free accommodation and transport and can purchase an apartment at building cost. Employees from both SOEs and DPEs show a high intention to be involved in reward policies and practices and want to have a say in managerial decisions with regard to rewards. At the same time, they are worried about the fairness of practices in setting these rewards and whether their involvement makes any difference. The next section will focus on career management from the employees' perspective.

Career management

Career management is a newly introduced concept in China. Employees are becoming educated and expect more from their employment. With a clear plan about their future careers, employees choose wisely and rationally in accepting jobs and developing their careers. Therefore, it is important for employers to adopt effective career management that increases employees' commitment and lowers their intention to leave. In this section, employee opinions on career management are illustrated.

In both SOEs and DPEs, it is found that not all employees are aware of career management practices in their companies (e.g., SOE4E1, SOE4E3, DPE1E2 and DPE6E1). In SOEs, employees would like to discuss with HR staff when they need assistance, but many employees remained uninformed about particular career management aspects in their companies. Employees evaluated different factors when they were planning their career with their current employers. SOE1E2 said: 'I am looking for stability in my life and work. Security in my job is my concern. I would be happy to have any chance to discuss my career with HR staff'. SOE3E2 also claimed: 'Career management is ambiguous to me. I think my career development within this organization is pre-set'. SOE1E3's perceptions were: 'It is competitive because we work on a project basis. I am concerned about my career but I am not informed about any formal career development'. SOE2E2 noted: 'There are many co-workers that are more senior than me. I am not sure when my chance will come up. HR staff updates us about new position or promotion opportunities from time to time. I am not sure whether they have any career management system'.

Operational employees in SOEs rarely find career development opportunities. SOE2E1 said: 'It is too difficult for me to have a career development plan. It is far from my reach. The cost of pursuing development [e.g. study after work] is too costly'. Other operational employees (e.g., DPE3E1 and DPE5E2) thought the best thing that could happen to them was being promoted to be in charge of an assembly line. They did not expect any future career development. PE3E1 claimed: 'I am tired after long hours of work. The only thing I want is having a good rest. It is a job rather than a career'.

In contrast, employees in DPEs that had established reputations and resources had more opportunities to access career management. DPE4E1 commented that 'our career management system is very complete. Our employee manual lists requirements for each position. We can also consult with HR staff for any further details and help customize individual career pathways'. DPE2E1 also claimed: 'I was informed about the career pathways [i.e. managerial and technical] available to us. Training before my commencement provides me with briefing information'.

In a number of DPEs, career management is perceived by employees as a promotion opportunity. For example, DPE1E1 said: 'On our bulletin board, there is a poster which draws out the structure of our organization. I think it is a way of showing how we can get promoted within this organization. In my opinion, it is very general as we have a number of functional departments and individuals have their own demands to be fulfilled'.

In addition, employees preferred to plan their career development by themselves and only sought help from HR specialists if needed. SOE1E1 and SOE1E2 agreed that they were informed about how they could follow a career pathway in this organization. SOE1E3 noted: 'I have my own plan about my career development in this company. I may ask HR for more advice if I need'. This opinion was shared among other employees from DPEs (e.g., DPE3E1 and DPE1E2). DPE4E1 said: 'We are encouraged to plan our future by ourselves. Career management is part of our training programs. If we are more skilled, the future is clearer'. However, this positive view was not shared by everyone, in particular among the operational employees who did not have a clear career plan and did not think it was necessary (i.e., employees from DPE3 and DPE5).

Many other employees wished to be informed about their career development. Employees in SOE1 (E1, E2 and E3) wanted to be informed about career development in this organization because jobs were important to them. A clear picture of the future helps them make correct choices to stay or leave. SOE2E2 admitted: 'It would be better if the company offered help with individual career management'. DPE1E1 added: 'If there is a career development system, the employees will be happy to know what their future looks like in this organization. The future would fit their expectations, they will want to stay; otherwise they won't'. The need for being informed is shared among employees across the various categories, such as entry-level employees (SOE2E4) and relative long-term employees (SOE3E1 and SOE4E3), with high expectations of the current employer.

The extent to which employees are informed about career development varies within the same business. For example, certain employees in DPE2 (DPE2E1 and DPE2E2) were better informed than others about career development practices and opportunities. They believed that careers needed to be planned systematically in accordance with the company's development. The help and resources provided by the company were meaningful to them, and they wanted to make good use of these resources. They pointed out that if the company helped them organize their future career, it would make them feel that they were taken care of. This would have a positive effect on their intention to stay, and they would work hard in return. For example, DPE4E2 stated: 'If we are shown a clear future career development in this organization, we would like to stay'. DPE6E1 responded: 'I want to develop within this organization. If I can get more help developing my career pathway, I will be more determined to stay'.

Other than future careers, fairness in career management procedures is a concern for employees. For example, SOE2E3 said: 'It is hard to choose freely in SOEs as the positions and number are set by policy. Being qualified for a position does not necessarily mean getting that job. Even if I have a clear career plan, I am not sure whether it is practical in reality'.

In summary, career management is beginning to attract the attention of employees in SOEs and DPEs as employees are becoming more educated. The employees interviewed realized that career management may make a difference to their lives if utilized systematically. Given the limitations of autonomy, employees in SOEs did not participate actively in career management, taking their preference for job security into account. They were reluctant to leave SOEs unless other opportunities were significantly better. They approached HR specialists for advice when needed. The responses from employees in DPEs on career management were similar to those of employees in SOEs. They agreed that becoming involved in career management increased the possibility of staying; however, career management was of little of use in retaining employees with clear future plans, especially those who wanted to run their own business. The next section will illustrate another relevant issue, namely employee retention from the employees' perspective.

Employee retention

According to managers' perspectives, retaining valuable employees remains a more challenging issue in DPEs than in SOEs. Managers implement HR practices in alignment with business strategies and other HR functions in order to retain as many employees as possible. From the employees' perspective, a number of factors are considered when they are making decisions on whether to stay or not. Employees from the sampled companies provided their opinions on the issue of retention policies and practices in their companies.

Employees in the sample SOEs were not aware of any retention practices and policies in their companies; however, most of them indicated that they would stay with their current employers. SOE1E2 explained: 'Most of my colleagues want to stay with this company, especially ladies. Jobs are secure here. I am not sure whether we have any retention practices because I have not thought of leaving yet'. SOE3E1 shared a similar view: 'I have been with this company since I graduated. I do not have any intention of leaving because I have not found any better offer. I bought a house in this city. The cost of relocation is high. I do not know whether we have a retention policy. One of my colleagues was asked to talk to HR staff before he wanted to quit. I have no idea what he was told and he did not disclose any details with us'.

Employees indicated that whether they should stay with their current employers is considered to be a personal issue. Employees do not discuss this problem with their colleagues in detail, especially the offers made by employers to retain them. SOE1E1 said: 'Marketing is a stressful job. Some of my colleagues planned to quit but in the end they stayed. I am not sure of the reasons for changing their minds. It may be due to the employee retention practices which I am not aware of'. Similarly, SOE3E3 said: 'As far as I know, there is no retention practice or policy which is publicly accessible to us. But I assume it can be discussed in private with the HR specialist'. SOE3E1 shared a similar view: 'I think employees will not know about the retention practices and policies unless they want to leave. It is better to discuss this privately as the reasons for leaving can be complicated and personal. On the other hand, I do not want my colleagues to know'.

Similarly to employees in SOEs, most employees from DPEs cannot identify employee retention policies and practices in their companies. Operational employees working in major manufacturing companies (DPE3 and DPE5) did not consider themselves to be the group of employees worth retaining by their employers. One employee from DPE3 (DPE3E1) said: 'I think they will only retain leaders on the assembly line. The leaders are good at their jobs and experienced. They can easily find others like me in the market. They will not bother retaining me. Drawn from this logic, if I can find a job which pays better, I will leave for sure'.

Employees' understanding of retention policies and practices in DPEs appeared to be different from that of managers. Most of them perceived retention practices to be an isolated set much like performance management practices. For managers, employee retention can be achieved by training, rewarding and providing career opportunities. Few employees thought retention practices could be implemented in other forms; one exception is the employee from DPE2 (DPE2E1), who noted, 'Rewards can be part of the retention policies as people will stay if they are satisfied. The main reason for leaving for my colleagues is underpayment. It is quite understandable because different people vary in their expectations'. DPE7E1 made a similar comment: 'We are understaffed. Managers make great efforts to retain us. Higher than average salaries is one of these methods'.

Reasons for leaving listed by employees were mainly personal, and most are not persuadable. DPE4E1 said: 'Most of the people who decided to leave did so due to imbalance between workload and salary. Even if the company has any retention practices, I doubt whether they will stay'. Another employee from DPE4 (DPE4E3) described what happened to his roommate: 'My previous roommate left because he could not get along well with his supervisors. It is beyond what HR specialists are capable of. It was impossible to fire the supervisors, so he left'. DPE2E2 mentioned that another possible reason for leaving is fairness in the workplace.

In SOEs, most employees do not see themselves as being influenced by employee retention issues as they do not have an intention to leave. In DPEs, employees who consider their positions to be interchangeable are not involved in retention issues at all. Other employees who are not aware of retention practices are rarely influenced. Retention practices have little effect on employees. In other words, employees who decide to stay will do so regardless of whether or not retention practices exist. Employees who intend to leave will leave even if retention practices are implemented.

According to employees, the reasons for staying are complicated and mixed:

a Job security, as claimed by SOE1E2: 'I want to work for this company in the future as the job is secured. The work pressure is not as much as in a private company'. SOE3E3 agreed: 'I would stay because my current job is secure and I am doing what I am interested in and good at. Whether there is a retention policy or not affects me significantly'.
b Workload, as SOE4E1 indicated: 'I will stay because I am quite satisfied with my current job. Workload is reasonable. It never occurs to me that I need to change my job'.
c Salary, as SOE2E1 claimed: 'My remuneration here is around average in this industry. I may leave in future, but it depends on what is offered'.
d Recognition of efforts, as SOE3E1 noted: 'I have been here for a long time. It matters that my contribution and effort is recognized by the company. Even if there is no particular retention policy, I would stay because

I am settling down in this city and do not want to move at the moment'. Employees from DPEs (notably, DPE1E2) also shared similar comments. One employee (DPE5E1) said: 'I guess only employees who have outstanding performance will be retained. I think the practices will not be revealed until the day I decide to leave. I expect that I will be retained when that day comes, which means my contribution and performance is recognized by them'.

e Reputation of company and promising future: employees from DPE4 agreed that they would stay based on the reputation of the company within the industry and the recognition of their educational program. In DPE7, current employees wanted to stay for the higher than average payment they received. They also stated that the uncertain but possibly promising future of this company was one of the reasons for them staying.

f Learning from the job, as DPE2E2 claimed: 'I do not have any intention of leaving as I made great efforts to get my job. I want to learn more from my job'.

In the employees' opinions, getting involved has positive effects on their motivation and commitment. For example, DPE1E1 said: 'Retention is not an isolated practice. It is the combination of rewarding, training and performance management. I do believe that our management team did an excellent job in this regard. I am quite motivated and feel I am a member of the team'. DPE2E4 agreed, saying: 'Getting involved and informed is always a positive signal sent from employers. To entry-level employees, we are taken care of and the company is concerned about us'.

To sum up this discussion, most of the employees in SOEs and DPEs were not aware of policies and practices of retaining valuable employees. Consistent with managers' responses, employees in SOEs showed a lower intention of leaving mainly because of job security and lower work pressure. In DPEs, employees were open to the possibility of leaving their current employers, and the reasons for leaving were complicated, including fairness and interpersonal relationships at work, as well as better pay and working conditions. Since most of the employees were not aware of practices and policies to retain them, the effect on employees is difficult to identify; however, employees from both SOEs and DPEs revealed that the reasons for them staying with their current companies included job security, reasonable workload, expectation of a promising future and recognition of their efforts at work.

Implications

Our interview results demonstrate that developing and implementing SHRM/HPWS among the Chinese indigenous companies remains a managerial responsibility. First, during the process of development and implementation, managers aligned HR policies and practices with business strategies. Employees indicated that they could observe the alignment between business strategies and HR practices being implemented. Second, since HR policies and practices are implemented by managers, these managers perceived the policies and practices to be effective. However, employees' perceptions were not exactly the same. Employees normally focused on HR policies and practices affecting them at an individual level, such as training, performance evaluation and reward policy, and the consequent influence on their well-being. Third, managers value organizational outcomes over individual outcomes, while employees care more about their own well-being, such as job satisfaction, fairness and trust relationships in the workplace.

The comparative analysis of the similarities and differences between managers' and employees' perceptions is meaningful and provides a unique opportunity to evaluate the adoption of SHRM/HPWS and the consequent influence on employees. A number of important lessons for developing workable and effective HR systems have been illustrated, such as fairness, trust relationships and a positive working environment which advocates open and free communication. Therefore, both processes, namely 'top-down' and 'bottom-up', as part of implementation of SHRM/HPWS, are crucial for eventual successful outcomes.

Contextual and possible moderating factors

Although the contextual or moderating factors are not the focus of this study, the existence of such factors plays a role during the implementation of SHRM/HPWS. The last question in the semi-structured interview invites interviewees to identify factors which influence the implementation of SHRM/HPWS. It covers external environmental factors (e.g., legislation), internal environmental factors (e.g., organizational culture) and future challenges. This section presents a brief discussion on these factors and the findings which may have meaningful indication for future study.

Both managers' and employees' responses often referred to the influence of traditional Chinese culture as well as organizational culture and identified these as important factors. With reference to organizational culture, a number of managers indicated that they made great efforts to create a working environment in which the company was seen as everyone's family (rooted in Chinese culture) and where 'open communication and innovation' were crucial elements for business success. By encouraging open communication, pressure on employees to voice their opinions is alleviated. Effective communication ensures that employees are aware of HR policies and practices implemented, as well as the rationales of implementation, both of which have positive effects on SHRM/HPWS implementation.

Legislation is often identified by managers as an important factor. The enforcement of labour laws and regulations emphasizes employee rights. Managers gradually become aware that they should pay more attention to employees' rights; however, they have also raised concerns that such protection is abused by employees in some cases. For example, employees are allowed to quit a job with short notice, which potentially increases the difficulties of finding new replacements.

The employees in this study are from different age groups. Employees in their early 20s like to take risks; they seek jobs with challenge, fun and better pay. They can therefore easily quit their jobs, find a new one and make an effort to adapt to the new working environment quickly. They also handle changes quickly in the workplace, including changes in HR policies and practices. In the managers' opinion, these employees in their early 20s are difficult to retain and are not afraid of arguing with their supervisors. Employees in their 30s are mostly skilled and experienced and are highly valued by employers. In their view, their sense of stability increases as they begin to think of settling down. They also realize the importance of career development and plan their career path carefully. They observe HR policies and practices implemented and then communicate with their supervisors in order to have a better understanding of the impact on their well-being. Employees in their 40s normally remain passive recipients of HR policies and practices. Managers perceive employees in this age group as difficult to communicate with because they are experienced and are not as open to changes as other age groups.

As reviewed in literature, gender can be a factor affecting employee perceptions and behaviours at work. Our interviews indicated that the majority of female employees preferred to work for SOEs because of the high level of job security and low work pressure. In managers' opinions, female employees are more obedient in comparison with male employees. Therefore, they accept and adapt to the changes of HR policies and practices quickly. Due to the limited time and scale of the fieldwork in China, many other important issues related to age, gender, educational background, work experiences and other employees' personal background were not investigated deeply; these constitute limitations of this research, and future research will cover these aspects in a more comprehensive manner.

Conclusion

This chapter has detailed the interview findings from managers' and employees' perspectives in Chinese indigenous companies in terms of the research objective and four key research questions through semi-structured interviews with both managers and employees.

A comparison was performed between the responses from SOEs and DPEs. This comparison was intended to illustrate similarities and differences in the adoption and implementation of HPWS in Chinese indigenous enterprises. The characteristics embedded in these two types of ownership enterprises affect how managers design and implement HR policies and practices. Employees from different ownership enterprises perceived and reacted to implemented HPWS differently. A comparison was also performed between managers and employees; this approach provides further understanding of the different perspectives regarding the adoption and implementation of SHRM/HPWS and the influence on employees.

In addition, this chapter provides sufficient evidence with which to address a number of key research questions. The interview findings also help identify relevant indicators and potential mediating relationships to be tested in the quantitative study presented in the next chapter. HPWS which encourage employee participation are proposed to influence trust between employees and managers. Mutual trust could lead to positive individual outcomes such as high job satisfaction and commitment to job/organization. Therefore, in the next chapter, the focus will be on a quantitative analysis in order to explore the potential relationships among these key aspects generated here and the mediating impact of trust between manager/supervisor and employees on the outcomes of employees' satisfaction and commitment. By doing so, we can further explore one of the key research questions, namely, 'What HRM systems can organizations develop to encourage positive attitudes of employees?'

References

Appelbaum, E. and Batt, R. 1994. *The new American workplace: Transforming work system in the United States.* Ithaca, NY: Cornell ILR Press.

Armstrong, C., Flood, P. C., Guthrie, J. P., Liu, W., Maccurtain, S. and Mkamwa, T. 2010. The impact of diversity and equality management on firm performance: Beyond high performance work systems. *Human Resource Management*, 49, 977–998.

Bae, J. and Lawler, J. J. 2000. Organizational and HRM strategies in Korea: Impact on firm performance in an emerging economy. *Academy of Management Journal*, 43, 502–517.

Batt, R. 2002. Managing customer services: Human resource practices, quit rates, and sales growth. *Academy of Management Journal*, 45, 587–597.

Evans, W. R. and Davis, W. D. 2005. High-performance work systems and organizational performance: The mediating role of internal social structure. *Journal of Management*, 31, 758–775.

Gould-Williams, J. 2003. The importance of HR practices and workplace trust in achieving superior performance: A study of public-sector organizations. *International Journal of Human Resource Management*, 14, 28–54.

Guest, D. E. and Conway, N. 2002. Communicating the psychological contract: An employer perspective. *Human Resource Management Journal*, 12, 22–38.

Guthrie, J. P. 2001. High-involvement work practices, turnover, and productivity: Evidence from New Zealand. *Academy of Management Journal*, 44, 180–190.

Huselid, M. A. 1995. The impact of human resource management practices on turnover, productivity, and corporate financial performance. *Academy of Management Journal*, 38, 635–672.

Ichniowski, C. and Shaw, K. 1999. The effects of human resource management systems on economic performance: An international comparison of US and Japanese plants. *Management Science*, 45, 704–721.

Lawler III, E. E. 1986. *High-involvement management.* San Francisco: Jossey-Bass.

Lepak, D. P. and Snell, S. A. 2002. Examining the human resource architecture: The relationships among human capital, employment, and human resource configurations. *Journal of Management*, 28, 517–543.

Liao, H., Toya, K., Lepak, D. P. and Hong, Y. 2009. Do they see eye to eye? Management and employee perspectives of high-performance work systems and influence processes on service quality. *Journal of Applied Psychology*, 94, 371–391.

Whitener, E. M. 2001. Do "high commitment" human resource practices affect employee commitment? A cross-level analysis using hierarchical linear modeling. *Journal of Management*, 27, 515–535.

Zacharatos, A., Barling, J. and Iverson, R. D. 2005. High-performance work systems and occupational safety. *Journal of Applied Psychology*, 90, 77–93.

5 The mediating role of trust

Survey results

Introduction

The previous chapter presented the findings of our study based on the semi-structured interview data. The managers and employees who participated in the interviews revealed that the implementation of HPWS affects their job satisfaction and turnover intention. In order to explore the potential relationships among the key aspects analyzed in the Stage One study, we demonstrate in the Stage Two study the mediating role of trust between manager/supervisor and employees within the context of implementation of HPWS. This approach is confirmatory in nature, with the aim of testing these relationships and tackling the research question of 'What HRM systems can organizations develop to encourage positive attitudes and intentions to stay?'

The next section begins with an explanation of the survey development, as informed by the interview findings discussed in chapter 4. A short summary of the data collection and analysis procedure will also be outlined, providing the context of this research. The following sections present the results drawn from the SEM technique, based on the analytical procedures recommended in the literature. SEM is increasingly being applied in social science and was selected because of its ability to estimate multiple relationships simultaneously, employ multiple indicators to measure the construct of interest and determine the extent-of-fit between the proposed model and the empirical data (Ullman et al., 2007). Goodness-of-fit was assessed with the sample data through a variety of fit indices. Due to the lack of consensus in literature about the best performing indices, different fit indices were used. Following the presentation of the SEM analysis, a brief discussion is provided and paves the way for the final discussion in the concluding chapter.

Development of the survey

The findings of the Stage One study indicated that employees were not aware of all HR policies and practices used by the organization. Employees demonstrated a high level of awareness of some HR policies and practices, such as job security, performance appraisals and rewards, while they showed relatively low levels of awareness on issues such as staffing, employee retention and to some degree career management.

The interview questions invited managers and employees to assess the level of employee participation as it is an important component of HPWS addressed in the literature. Managers predominantly believed that their subordinates/employees were involved in implementing the HPWS. They described how employees were provided opportunities to participate. However, employees' responses illustrated that employees were not actively involved. Some of them felt reluctant to participate or even avoided participation due to lack of fairness and possible adverse effects from voicing their opinions. Regardless of the extent to which employees were involved in the implementation process, they admitted that their level of participation influenced their interpretation of HR policies, practices and even business strategies. In other words, high levels of participation enabled employees to obtain information and form their interpretation of HR policies, practices and business strategies.

The relationship between employees and their managers, especially their immediate supervisors, played a critical role during the implementation of HPWS. Employees formed perceptions of their supervisors' capabilities based on the supervisors' past decisions. Employees indicated that if their supervisors showed them care and respect, gave employees more autonomy at work and looked after their interests, employees tended to develop and place high levels of trust in their supervisors. Such mutual trust between managers/supervisors and employees potentially strengthened employees' attachment to their current employers and increased their job satisfaction.

Additionally, the implementation of HR practices created a harmonic, equitable and innovative atmosphere. Employees indicated that they were affected by the working environment. They preferred to work in a company where they felt comfortable and were treated as a 'family' member.

The qualitative study provides rich information on the HPWS practices, how such practices are implemented and the effects on employee attitudes and behaviour at work. The study confirmed the influence of HPWS on employee perceptions of HR related issues. It also confirmed the influence that opportunities to participate have on the way individuals interpret business strategies and HR policies and practices. These findings and the relationship between the factors (i.e., HPWS, trustworthiness, job satisfaction and turnover intention) are interwoven in the hypothesized model shown in Figure 5.1.

The measurements for the Stage Two study were adopted from literature and refined on the basis of qualitative outcomes. The first part of the Stage Two study focused on employee perception and evaluated how HPWS were perceived. The second part evaluated managers' trustworthiness as perceived by employees. Last, the third part assessed employee outcomes (i.e., job satisfaction and turnover intention), consistent with the aims of the current study to incorporate employees into HPWS studies.

Thus, the final version of the survey examined two sets of latent variables: one exogenous variable (perceived HPWS) and one endogenous (trustworthiness), as

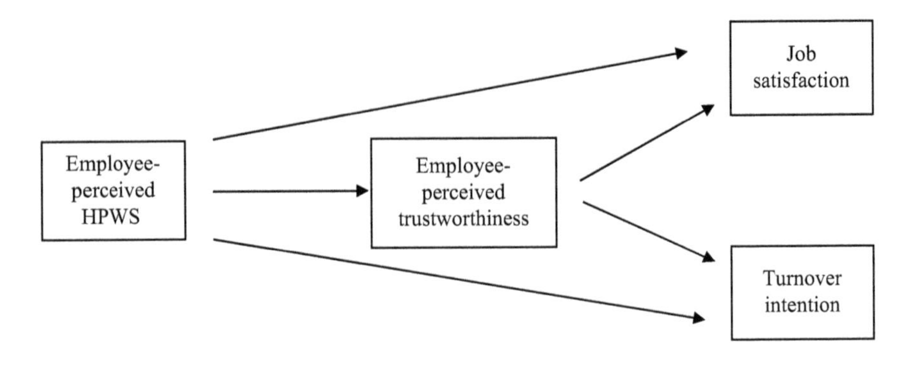

Figure 5.1 Hypothesized research model

well as the related outcomes (job satisfaction and turnover intentions). Latent variables are not directly observed; rather, they are measured based on the observable variables, by way of the covariance among two or more indicators (Kline, 2005). Research in psychology and other social sciences is often concerned with questions that are more subjective than questions posed in natural science research, such as questions related to perception, knowledge and sense. A latent variable elicits two or more observable items, the sum of which allows a conclusion about the construct (Cohen et al., 2013). The survey was developed in English and translated into Chinese by using conventional translation/back-translation technique. This was done to ensure reliability and validity (Behling and Law, 2000).

As introduced in chapter 1, this research surveyed employees at different time points, which facilitated exploration of the causal chain. The employees received two questionnaires – the first survey examined employee background information, the independent variables (HPWS) and potential mediating variables (trustworthiness), and the second survey examined the dependent variables (job satisfaction and turnover intention). The two surveys were sent out with a one-month interval (i.e., November 2014 and January 2015 respectively).

Data screening

Prior to analysis, data were examined for accuracy of data entry, missing values and assumptions of the multivariate analysis. The primary objective of this process was to ensure that the dataset was accurate, was appropriate and did not significantly violate the assumptions associated with SEM. Data were checked to detect any entry errors or out-of-range values. A few errors were found and corrected after a review of the hardcopy survey.

Constructs related to perceived HPWS and perceived trustworthiness had missing values in fewer than 5 percent of cases. Given that the sample size in this quantitative study was large (i.e., more than 900), the problems associated with missing values were not serious (Tabachnick and Fidell, 2007). An examination of these cases revealed that no significant pattern was visible. Moreover, the survey was divided into two parts for EFA and CFA respectively. The temporal separation reduces the likelihood of intentional omission of scores due to common source bias (Podsakoff et al., 2003).

SEM data analysis requires multivariate normality of the observed data. In this research, multivariate normality of the variables was tested by obtaining a Mahalanobis distance, which is the distance of a particular case in the dataset from the centroid of the remaining cases. The centroid is the point created by the means of the variables under investigation (Tabachnick and Fidell, 2007). The Mahalanobis distance follows a Chi-square distribution when the degree of freedom is more than 10. A case is a multivariate outlier if the probability associated with its Mahalanobis distance is 0.001 or less. One of the ways of handling multivariate outliers is deleting outliers (Barrett, 2007). Although outliers are handled by obtaining Mahalanobis distance, the multivariate normality is rarely satisfied in real-life data. However, not meeting this requirement is not problematic (Chou and Bentler, 1995). An estimation method, such as maximum likelihood (ML) estimation, has been found to be fairly robust to violation of normality (Chou and Bentler, 1995). In this sense, maximum likelihood parameter estimates with standard errors and a mean-adjusted Chi-square test statistic (MLM) are used in this research as estimation method. According to Byrne (2012), if the data are multivariate normal, differences between the Chi-square values should be minimal. An indicator is the scaling correction factor. If the value of the scaling correction factor is larger than 1 and there is a large discrepancy between the Chi-square values, the data are multivariate non-normal. Under this circumstance, the adoption of MLM rather than ML is recommended (Byrne, 2012). The scaling correction factors for the variables were larger than 1. These parameters suggested that multivariate non-normality presented in the dataset. As a consequence, the MLM was adopted to analyze data, which was a reasonably robust to modest violation of normality (Byrne, 2012; Hu and Bentler, 1999).

In summary, 1,196 questionnaires were distributed, and 956 were collected, reflecting an 80 percent response rate. An examination of outliers and missing values among collected questionnaires revealed that 49 cases were deleted (14 outlying cases and 35 missing value cases), leaving 907 cases for further analysis. Of these 907 cases, 245 cases were from SOEs, while 662 cases were from DPEs. Samples in each ownership group were further randomly divided into half for a factor analysis. The first half was subjected to an exploratory factor analysis, and the second half was used in a confirmatory factor analysis.

Factor structures for SOE and DPE samples

In this research, multivariate non-normality exists in the dataset and does not severely violate multivariate normality (e.g., scaling correction factor = 1.1374). Therefore, maximum likelihood was used to extract factors as suggested (Fabrigar et al., 1999). Factor extraction removes variance common to sets of variables from the original matrix of association. After the first factor has been extracted, a residual matrix remains. A second factor is then extracted from the residual matrix to explain as much of the remaining variance among the variables as possible. The process continues until noteworthy variance can no longer be explained by factors.

Variables are factored; however, not all factors substantially contribute to the overall solution or are interpretable. Given that the goal of EFA is to retain the fewest possible factors while explaining the highest variance of the observed variables, it is critical that correct numbers of factors are retained. To determine the number of factors, the eigenvalue > 1 rule is used. It is a default option in most statistics packages and the most widely used decision rule (Thompson and Daniel, 1996).

In the EFA, factor structures (i.e., perceived HPWS, trustworthiness, job satisfaction and turnover intention) were examined. Each of the factor structures was examined following the procedures described earlier, as the eigenvalue > 1 rule was first used to determine the number of factors. The correlations between items and the factors then were examined, and the items with above 0.4 loadings were kept. Finally, goodness-of-fit statistics and Cronbach's alpha were assessed and calculated for reliability.

Perceived HPWS

A 28-item scale from the Sun et al. (2007) study was utilized to measure employees' perception of HPWS in organizations. Items from interviews in the Stage One study were revised according to suggestions from employees and managers to assure relevance of items.

In the SOE samples, HPWS items were subjected to EFA using maximum likelihood extraction with an oblique rotation; 12 items from this process were retained and loaded on four factors representing staffing, career management, performance management and participation. For each factor, items had loadings above 0.4 on primary factors (Stevens, 2012). Cronbach's alpha for the 12 items was 0.875.

In the DPE samples, EFA procedure was repeated on HPWS items; 11 items were retained. These items were loaded on four factors: namely, staffing, career management, performance management and participation. For each factor, items had loadings above 0.4 on primary factors. Cronbach's alpha for the 11 items was 0.873.

Perceived trustworthiness

The 17-item trustworthiness scale suggested by Mayer and Davis (1999) was utilized. This measurement is a 17-item scale which measures the perceived ability, integrity and benevolence of management in organizations. Again, relevance of the items was confirmed by the employee and manager interviews in the Stage One study. Items were also subjected to EFA using maximum likelihood extraction.

In SOE samples, seven items measuring trustworthiness of management were retained. These items were loaded on three factors, representing ability, integrity and benevolence of management, in consistency with expectations. For each factor, items had loadings above 0.4 on primary factors. Cronbach's alpha for the seven items was 0.923.

In DPE samples, trustworthiness items were subjected to EFA in accordance with the procedure described earlier; 10 items were retained, representing three factors as expected. Cronbach's alpha for the ten items was 0.940.

Job satisfaction and turnover intention

Job satisfaction items were included from Hackman and Oldham's (1980) scale; 12 items were subjected to EFA. From the SOE samples, five items were retained to reflect general satisfaction with work, and from the DPE samples, five items were retained. Cronbach's alphas for measurement items related to job satisfaction in SOEs and DPEs were 0.810 and 0.789 respectively. With regard to turnover intention, the three-item scale suggested by Irving et al. (1997) was used. As with items for HPWS and trustworthiness, items for job satisfaction and turnover intention were revised according to suggestions from employees and managers from interviews in the Stage One study to assure relevance. In particular, as suggested by employees and managers, items for turnover intention were revised using positive words which were intended to make respondents feel more comfortable about answering questions. In SOEs and DPEs, measurement items were subjected to EFA, and two items were retained. Cronbach's alphas for measurement items for outcomes were 0.401 and 0.476 respectively.

While a minimum of three of four indicators per latent variable was previously the requirement for testing a single common factor in isolation, scholars have increasingly challenged this perception. Hayduk and Glaser (2000) fiercely argued that, with many latent variables and reasonable consideration of latent-to-latent effects, two indicators or a single indicator per factor are sufficient. Their argument is supported by Boomsma (2000), who stated that large sample size compensates for a small number of indicators per factor ratio. Therefore, two items are used for turnover intention in the current study.

Measurement model for SOE and DPE samples

EFA gives a low-dimensional description of high-dimensional data but is not based on a uniquely identifiable model. It finds factors that best reproduce the variables under the maximum likelihood conditions (Gorsuch and Hao, 1993). Using a maximum likelihood exploratory program, it leads to a hypothesized number of underlying factors which can be specified, and the goodness-of-fit of the resulting solution can be tested (Anderson and Gerbing, 1988). This point is the demarcation of the move to CFA, which is typically driven by theoretical expectations to develop the structure of the data. It is used in situations where knowledge of the dimensionality of the variables under study is based on a theory or empirical

Table 5.1 Reliability analysis for SOE samples

Construct	*Number of items*	*Cronbach's alpha*
Perceived HPWS	12	0.875
Trustworthiness	7	0.923
Job Satisfaction	5	0.810
Turnover Intention	2	0.401

Table 5.2 Reliability analysis for DPE samples

Construct	*Number of items*	*Cronbach's alpha*
Perceived HPWS	11	0.873
Trustworthiness	10	0.940
Job Satisfaction	5	0.789
Turnover Intention	2	0.476

findings (Brown, 2006). The measurement model is first tested to provide a confirmatory assessment of convergent validity and discriminant validity (Campbell and Fiske, 1959). After convergent and discriminant validity is confirmed, the test of the structural model is performed, which then constitutes a confirmatory assessment of nomological validity (Campbell, 1960). The conjunctional use of measurement model and structural model enables a comprehensive and confirmatory assessment of the hypothesized model (Bentler, 1978) for the current study.

Perceived HPWS

Firstly, a CFA was performed on the hypothesized measurement model pertaining to the employee-perceived HPWS. The CFA measurement model for HPWS in the SOE samples, indicated a poor fit with χ^2 = 116.208, df = 48, RMSEA (root mean square error of approximation) = 0.108, CFI (comparative fit index) = 0.928, TLI (Tucker-Lewis Index) = 0.900 and SRMR (standardized root mean square residual) = 0.063. All indicators loaded significantly on their respective construct ranging from 0.562 to 0.953. In this study, a second order CFA model was also tested.

A second order construct is seen as a latent model in which the dimension serves as an indicator (Law et al., 1998). It is suggested that it is appropriate to use scores from existing sub-scales as indicators of a higher order construct (Hall et al., 1999). Based on the relevance and integration of HPWS dimensions, perceived HPWS is conceived as a higher order construct (Beltrán-Martín et al., 2008), comprising staffing, internal mobility, performance management and participation. The measurement of HPWS was tested and established with four factors the structure of which was identified. The Chi-square difference was calculated between the first order and second order CFA models since the models were nested. The model fit statistics for the second order was found to be identical to those of the first order CFA. However, in the second order CFA model, the first order factors were found to be highly loaded onto the second order factors, with factor loadings ranging from 0.453 to 0.908. The proportions of variance in the first order factors explained by the second order were 0.206, 0.242, 0.679 and 0.824 respectively. Therefore, a second order CFA model for HPWS was considered appropriate in the current study.

The CFA procedure was repeated for the DPE samples. The CFA of HPWS demonstrated a poor fit with χ^2 = 129.952, *df* = 36, RMSEA = 0.089, CFI = 0.959, TLI = 0.937 and SRMR = 0.045. All indicators loaded significantly on their respective construct ranging from 0.624 to 0.930. A second order CFA model was also tested for the DPE samples. The results improved and demonstrated a marginal fit with χ^2 = 130.433, *df* = 38, RMSEA = 0.086, CFI = 0.960, TLI = 0.942 and SRMR = 0.045. The second order factor CFA model established that the first order factors loaded significantly onto the second order factors of HPWS. The factor loadings ranged from 0.424 to 0.841. The proportions of variance in the first order factors explained by the second order were 0.180, 0.261, 0.616 and 0.707 respectively.

Trustworthiness

The CFA of trustworthiness in the SOE sample achieved fit with χ^2 = 102.377, *df* = 51, RMSEA = 0.091, CFI = 0.962, TLI = 0.951 and SRMR = 0.050. All indicators loaded significantly on their respective construct ranging from 0.703 to 0.927. Similar to HPWS, a second order CFA model was tested for

Table 5.3 Second order factor loadings on HPWS and R^2 in SOE samples

	Factor loadings	R^2
Staffing	0.453	0.206
Internal Mobility	0.492	0.242
Performance	0.824	0.679
Participation	0.908	0.824

Table 5.4 Second order factor loadings on HPWS and R^2 in DPE samples

	Factor loadings	R^2
Staffing	0.424	0.180
Internal Mobility	0.511	0.261
Performance	0.785	0.616
Participation	0.841	0.707

Table 5.5 Second order factor loadings on trustworthiness and R^2 in SOE samples

	Factor loadings	R^2
Ability	0.851	0.727
Benevolence	0.948	0.856
Integrity	0.941	0.898

Table 5.6 Second order factor loadings on trustworthiness and R^2 in DPE samples

	Factor loadings	R^2
Ability	0.808	0.653
Benevolence	0.945	0.893
Integrity	0.941	0.885

trustworthiness; it consisted of three factors, which meant its structure was identified. The results demonstrated a good fit with χ^2 = 73.961, *df* = 49, RMSEA = 0.065, CFI = 0.982, TLI = 0.975 and SRMR = 0.026. The factor loadings of first order factors on the second order factors ranged from 0.851 to 0.948. The proportions of variance in the first order factors explained by the second order were 0.727, 0.856 and 0.898 respectively.

The CFA procedure was repeated in the DPE samples. The CFA of trustworthiness demonstrated marginal fit with χ^2 = 347.793, *df* = 101, RMSEA = 0.086, CFI = 0.953, TLI = 0.944 and SRMR = 0.037. All indicators loaded significantly on their respective construct ranging from 0.775 to 0.909. In the second order factor CFA model for DPE samples, the first order factors were found to be significantly loaded onto the second order factor. The factor loadings ranged from 0.808 to 0.945. The proportions of variance in the first order factors explained by the second order were 0.653, 0.893 and 0.885 respectively.

Job satisfaction and turnover intention

The CFA of job satisfaction in the SOE samples demonstrated poor fit with χ^2 = 3.842, *df* = 5, RMSEA = 0.000, CFI = 01.000, TLI = 1.000 and SRMR = 0.019. All indicators loaded significantly on a single factor ranging from 0.516 to 0.850. In DPEs, the CFA of job satisfaction in SOEs demonstrated poor fit with χ^2 = 90.677, *df* = 14, RMSEA = 0.129, CFI = 0.891, TLI = 0.837 and SRMR = 0.057. All indicators loaded significantly on a single factor ranging from 0.510 to 0.699.

The CFA of turnover intention in the SOEs demonstrated poor fit with χ^2 = 3.702, *df* = 1, RMSEA = 0, CFI = 0.948, TLI = 1.000 and SRMR = 0.000. Indicators loaded significantly on a single factor ranging as 0.581 to 0.672

respectively. In DPEs, $\chi^2 = 0$, df = 1, RMSEA = 0, CFI = 0.979, TLI = 1.000 and SRMR = 0.000. Indicators loaded significantly on a single factor ranging from 0.677 to 0.675 respectively.

Construct reliability and validity

Prior to the structural analysis of the relationships among latent variables, the scores obtained for the survey items should be proven to be valid and reliable. Construct reliability was assessed by examining composite reliability. The reliability test determined the extent of internal consistency for the measurement of the latent variables studied in this research. As Raykov and Shrout (2002) stated, the conventional Cronbach's alpha is subject to the assumption of constrained factor loadings and error variance.

The content validity was ensured by extensive review of the literature, the scientific design of the survey measurement and exploration in the qualitative stage prior to conducting surveys (Kocabasoglu et al., 2007). As for the validity of observed indicators, Diamantopoulos and his colleagues (2000) discussed the magnitude and significance of the loadings between the observed indicator and the associated latent variables. All the standardized loadings coefficients were above 0.500 (Hair, 1998) and significantly positive, thus lending support for the validity construct. Specifically, in the measurement model for perceived HPWS, the relationships between each item and its respective construct were all statistically significant, with standardized coefficients ranging from 0.440 to 0.914 for SOEs and from 0.624 to 0.930 for DPEs. This established the posited relationships between the indicators and constructs and, subsequently, the convergent validity and uni-dimensionality (Anderson and Gerbing, 1988; Kline, 2005). Similarly, the relationships between each item and its respective construct were all statistically significant, with standardized coefficients ranging from 0.851 to 0.948 in SOEs and ranging from 0.775 to 0.909 in DPEs for trustworthiness, from 0.516 to 0.850 in SOEs and from 0.510 to 0.699 in DPEs for job satisfaction and from 0.581 to 0.672 in SOEs and from 0.677 to 0.675 in DPEs for turnover intention.

Thus, in the measurement models concerning perceived HPWS, perceived trustworthiness, job satisfaction and turnover intention, the observed indicators demonstrated adequate reliability and validity in order to measure the respective latent factors, consistent with the theoretical expectations.

Structural model: hypothesis testing and alternative models

The previous section reported the measurement model pertaining to HPWS, trustworthiness, job satisfaction and turnover intention. These were tested to ensure construct validity, in preparation for use in the structural model. The statistics suggested a reasonable fit with the data in SOEs and DPEs respectively. This section discusses the structural model analysis and determines the path relationships among the latent variables for SOEs and DPEs separately. The goodness-of-fit between the hypothesized model and the sample data is reported, thus paving the way for a detailed analysis of the individual hypotheses.

To examine the antecedents and consequences, structural equation models were estimated using Mplus. The model shown in Figure 5.1 includes: a) direct effects of the perceived HPWS on job satisfaction and turnover intention; b) direct effects of perceived HPWS on perceived trustworthiness; and c) effects of trust on job satisfaction and turnover intention. To do this, models were estimated and statistically compared.

SOE sample: test of the structural model including mediation

The study received 245 valid questionnaires from employees in SOEs. Table 5.7 presents descriptive statistics and correlations amongst the variables used in model comparisons and hypothesis testing. To assess the hypothesized models and determine the likelihood of additional theoretical models, a series of nested structural models were estimated. A model is said to be nested within another model when its set of freely estimated parameters is a subset of those estimated in the saturated structural model (Anderson and Gerbing, 1988).

Model A is the hypothesized model illustrated in Figure 5.1. This model includes all the direct and indirect effects of HPWS on job satisfaction and turnover intention. In SOEs, this 'saturated' model accounted for the data reasonably well (χ^2 = 544.094, *df* = 286; RMSEA = 0.061, CFI = 0.928, TLI = 0.919). Model B is identical to Model A, except that the direct effects of perceived HPWS on job satisfaction are omitted. The Chi-square difference between these models is an overall test of the direct effects of the perceived HPWS on job satisfaction. As shown in Table 5.8, the difference was 50.112, which was significant at 1 degree of freedom. It appears that the direct effect of HPWS on job satisfaction is important and should not be omitted. The AIC (Akaike information criterion) score assesses the degree of parsimony of competing models and is applicable for cross-validation. Based on AIC, Model A enjoys better goodness-of-fit indices with lower AIC (AIC = 19222.817) than Model B (AIC = 19278.007).

Model C is identical to Model A but the effects of perceived HPWS on turnover intention were omitted. The Chi-square difference between Model C and Model A was 38.44, which was highly significant at 1 degree of freedom, indicating that the effects of the perceived HPWS on turnover intention made an important contribution to the overall fit of the model and should not be omitted. In terms of AIC, Model A (AIC = 19222.817) is lower than Model C (AIC = 19264.125).

Model D (AIC = 19316.188) is also the same as the saturated model, except that the effects of HPWS on trust were excluded. The Chi-squared difference between these models was 88.164, which was significant at 2 degrees of freedom. This indicates that the relationship between trust and job satisfaction contributes to the fit of the overall model; these paths should not be omitted.

Model E (AIC = 19309.444) examined the indirect effects of trust on job satisfaction. It is identical to Model A, except that the direct effects of trust on job satisfaction were omitted. The Chi-square difference between these models, as shown in Table 5.8, was 79.795, which was significant at 1 degree of freedom. Thus, it appears that trust has an impact on job satisfaction.

Model F (AIC = 19273.473) is the same as Model A, except that the effects of trust on turnover intention were removed. The Chi-square difference between Model F and Model A was 47.087, which was highly significant at 1 degree of freedom, indicating that trust influences turnover intention and should not be omitted.

Based on the comparison, Model A was accepted with empirical justification (Yuan and Bentler, 2004). A comparison between nested models is illustrated in Table 5.8.

Following the mainstream recommendations in the SEM literature (McDonald and Ho, 2002), the fit measures and path parameters of Model A are summarized in Figure 5.2. The results associated with the fit indices were mixed, with RMSEA = 0.061; the other goodness-of-fit indices indicated that model achieved good fit (χ^2 = 544.094, *df* = 286, CFI = 0.928, TLI = 0.919 and SRMR = 0.076).

R-squared value represents the proportion of variance in each observed variable accounted for by its related factor. In the hypothesized model in SOEs, all observed variables are adequately explained with R-squared values ranging from 0.087 to 0.893. In the case of latent variables, these are explained by their corresponding second order factors ranging from 0.191 to 0.921.

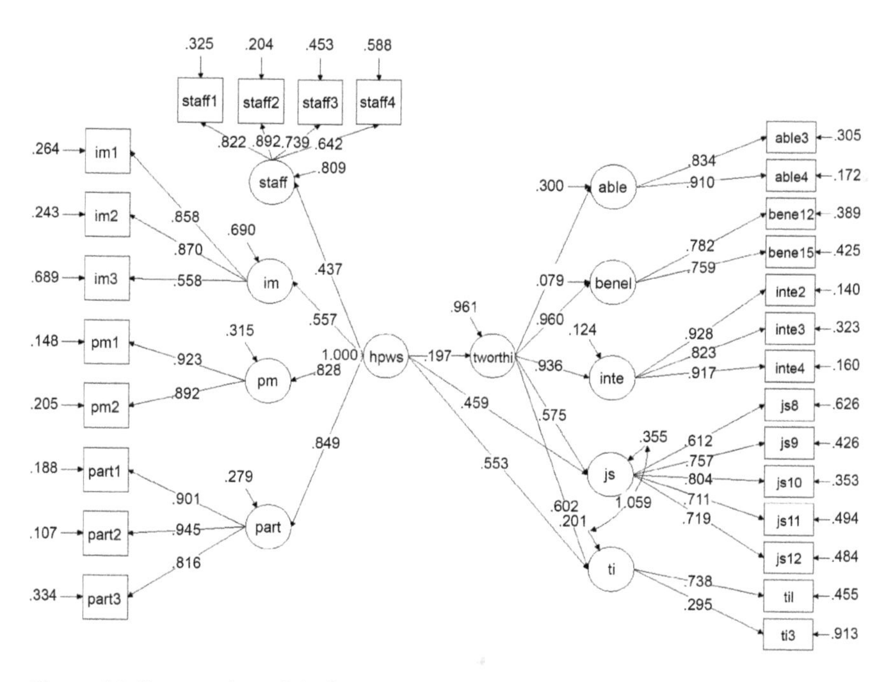

Figure 5.2 Structural model of SOEs

Table 5.7 Descriptive statistics and correlations for SOE samples

	SD	*Mean*	*1*	*2*	*3*	*4*	*5*	*6*	*7*	*8*	*9*	*10*
Staffing	1.082	0.000										
Internal Mobility	1.586	0.000	0.243									
Performance	1.421	0.000	0.362	0.461								
Participation	1.506	0.000	0.371	0.473	0.703							
HPWS	0.472	0.000	0.437	0.557	0.828	0.849						
Ability	1.270	0.000	0.072	0.092	0.136	0.140	0.165					
Benevolence	1.032	0.000	0.082	0.205	0.156	0.160	0.189	0.803				
Integrity	1.262	0.000	0.080	0.203	0.152	0.156	0.184	0.783	0.898			
Trustworthiness	1.062	0.000	0.086	0.110	0.163	0.167	0.197	0.837	0.960	0.936		
Job Satisfaction	0.924	0.000	0.250	0.319	0.474	0.486	0.572	0.557	0.638	0.623	0.665	
Turnover Intention	1.134	0.000	0.293	0.374	0.556	0.570	0.671	0.594	0.682	0.665	0.711	1.000

Table 5.8 SOE model comparison

Model	*Substantive interpretation*	*Goodness of fit*		*Chi-square differences*			*RMSEA*	*CI*		*CFI*	*TLI*	*SRMR*	*AIC*
		$\chi 2$	*df*	$\chi 2$	*df*	*p* value		Lower	Higher				
A	Full model	544.094	286				0.061	0.053	0.068	0.928	0.919	0.076	19222.817
B	Full model w/o JS–HPWS relationship	594.206	287	50.112	1	1.45216E-12	0.066	0.059	0.074	0.915	0.904	0.102	19278.007
C	Full model w/o TI–HPWS relationship	582.534	287	38.440	1	5.64632E-10	0.065	0.057	0.072	0.918	0.907	0.087	19264.125
D	Full model w/o Trust–HPWS relationship	632.258	288	88.164	2	7.16854E-20	0.070	0.062	0.077	0.905	0.892	0.121	19316.188
E	Full model w/o Trust–JS relationship	623.889	287	79.795	1	4.15342E-19	0.069	0.062	0.077	0.907	0.894	0.117	19309.444
F	Full model w/o Trust–TI relationship	591.181	287	47.087	1	6.79046E-12	0.066	0.058	0.073	0.916	0.905	0.095	19273.473

Note: JS: job satisfaction; TI: turnover intention.

Hypothesis testing using SOE samples

As discussed prior, the structural model (Model A) appeared to fit the sample data adequately, thus making it appropriate for hypothesis testing. With specific reference to the process applied to employee perceptions of job satisfaction, Hypothesis 1 proposes that the relationship between employee perceptions of the adoption of HPWS is positively related to employee job satisfaction. The results demonstrated a standardized coefficient of 0.459, SE = 0.058, $p < 0.001$, which supports the positive linkage between perceived HPWS and job satisfaction.

Hypothesis 2 assumes the negative relationship between employee perceptions of the adoption of HPWS and employee turnover intention. The items were written using positive words, thus indicating employees' intentions to stay in their current companies. The results demonstrated a standardized coefficient of 0.553, SE = 0.090, $p < 0.001$. Therefore, Hypothesis 2 was supported.

Hypothesis 3 was developed to examine the effect of employee perceptions of the adoption of HPWS and how these are positively related to their perception of management's trustworthiness. The results demonstrated a standardized coefficient of 0.197, SE = 0.076, $p < 0.01$. Hypothesis 3 was supported.

Hypothesis 4 postulated a positive relationship between employee perceptions of management's trustworthiness and employee job satisfaction. The result demonstrated a standardized coefficient of 0.575, SE = 0.062, $p < 0.001$. The positive relation between trustworthiness and employee job satisfaction was confirmed.

Hypothesis 5 examined the negative relationship between employee perceptions of management's trustworthiness and employee turnover intention. As pointed out earlier, these items were written using positive words, indicating employees' intention of staying in their current companies. The result demonstrated a standardized coefficient of 0.602, SE = 0.086, $p < 0.001$. This hypothesis was supported.

In order to investigate whether trustworthiness mediates the relation between HPWS and job satisfaction, the mediating effect was tested using the bootstrapping technique provided by Mplus 7.0. Bootstrapping, a non-parametric resampling procedure, is increasingly being advocated to supplement traditional statistical approaches (such as the Sobel test) to assess mediation. It overcomes the major limitations of traditional approaches because normality of the sampling distribution of the indirect effects is not assumed (MacKinnon et al., 2002). In the current study, bias-corrected bootstrapping confidence intervals were obtained based on 5,000 bootstrap samples. In the structural model, the standardized indirect effect of trust on job satisfaction was 0.221, with bootstrapping 95 percent confidence intervals at 0.042 and 0.447. Zero was not contained in the confidence intervals, and the mediating relationship was supported. The bootstrapping strategy was applied again to assess the mediation role of trust between perceived HPWS and turnover intention. The standardized indirect effects of trust on turnover intention was 0.283, with bootstrapping 95 percent confidence intervals at 0.053 and 0.551. Zero was not contained in the confidence intervals, and therefore the mediation role of trust between HPWS and turnover intention was supported.

DPE sample: test of the structural model using mediation

In this research 662 questionnaires were received from employees in the DPEs sampled. The descriptive statistics and correlations used are demonstrated in Table 5.9. The fit measures and path parameters of the structural models in DPEs are calculated by following the same procedure of testing the structural model in SOEs. Figure 5.3 presents the original structural model in which trustworthiness of managers as perceived by employees in the workplace mediated the relationship between HPWS and outcomes (i.e., job satisfaction and turnover intention). The findings also demonstrate that trustworthiness is positively related to outcomes. The results associated with the fit indices were mixed with RMSEA = 0.055; the other goodness-of-fit indices indicated that the model achieved a good fit (χ^2 = 1019.657, *df* = 337, CFI = 0.933, TLI = 0.924 and SRMR = 0.067).

The standardized model results demonstrate that parameter estimates of the hypothesized model exhibit the correct sign and size and are consistent with the underlying theory. Covariance or correlation matrices from which parameter estimates are taken are positive definite, and no out-of-range values are found.

In DPEs, the 'saturated' model (Figure 5.1) accounted for the data reasonably well (χ^2 = 1019.657, *df* = 337, RMSEA = 0.055, CFI = 0.933 and TLI = 0.924).

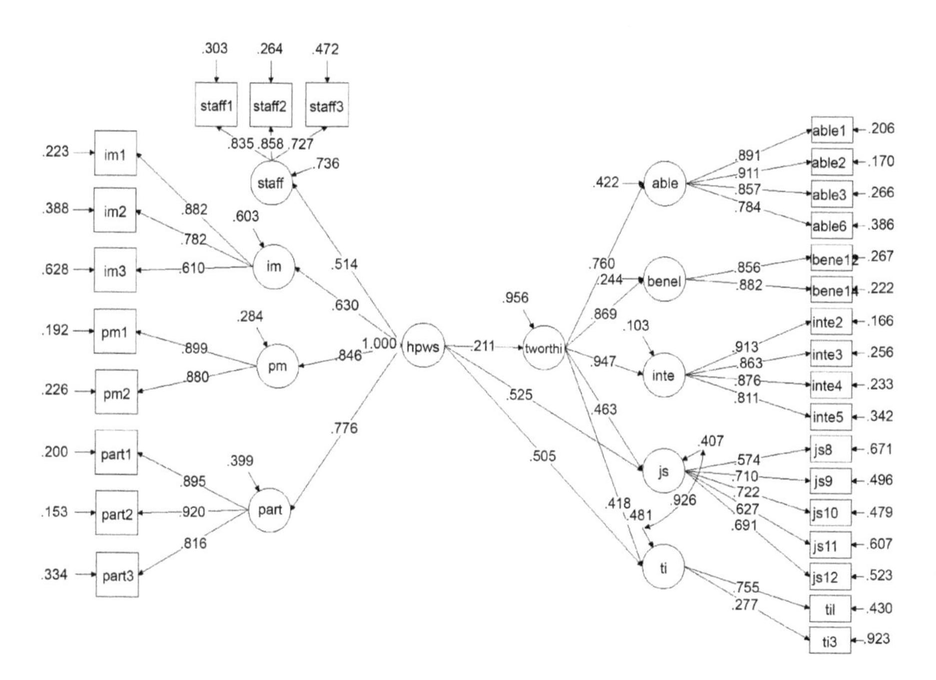

Figure 5.3 Structural model of DPEs

Model B is identical to Model A, except that the link between perceived HPWS and job satisfaction is omitted. The Chi-square differences between these models are an overall test of the direct effects of the perceived HPWS on job satisfaction. As shown in Table 5.10, the difference was 130.615 (significant at 1 degree of freedom). Consequently, the direct effect of HPWS on job satisfaction is important and should not be omitted. Based on AIC, Model A enjoys better goodness-of-fit indices with lower AIC (AIC = 55531.647) than Model B (AIC = 55688.455). The AIC score assesses the degree of parsimony of competing models and is applicable for cross-validation.

Model C is identical to Model A, excluding the effects of perceived HPWS on turnover intention. The Chi-square difference between Model C and Model A was 65.106, which was highly significant at 1 degree of freedom; this result indicates that the effects of the perceived HPWS on turnover intention made an important contribution to the overall fit of the model and should not be omitted. In terms of AIC, Model A (AIC = 55531.647) is lower than Model C (AIC = 55608.514).

Model D (AIC = 55670.341) is the same as the saturated model, except that the effects of HPWS on trust were omitted. The Chi-square difference between these models was 88.164, which was significant at 2 degrees of freedom. Therefore, it indicates that the relationship of trust to job satisfaction contributes to the fit of the overall model; these paths should not be omitted.

Model E (AIC = 55667.623) examined the indirect effects of trust on job satisfaction. It is identical to Model A, except that the direct effects of trust on job satisfaction were omitted. The Chi-square difference between these models, as shown in the Table 5.10, was 115.122, which was significant at 1 degree of freedom. Thus, it appears that trust has an impact on job satisfaction.

Model F (AIC = 55592.720) is the same as Model A, except that the effects of trust on turnover intention were removed. The Chi-square difference between Model F and Model A was 52.747, which was highly significant at 1 degree of freedom, thus indicating that trust influences turnover intention and should not be omitted.

The statistics for model comparison are summarized in Table 5.10. Based on the comparison, Model A was accepted with empirical justification (Yuan and Bentler, 2004). Following the mainstream recommendations in the SEM literature (McDonald and Ho, 2002), the fit measurements and path parameters of Model A are illustrated in Figure 5.3. The results associated with the fit indices were mixed with RMSEA = 0.055; the other goodness-of-fit indices indicated that the model achieved good fit (χ^2 = 1019.657, *df* = 337, CFI = 0.933, TLI = 0.924 and SRMR = 0.067).

Again, the R-squared value represents the proportion of variance in each observed variable accounted for by its related factor. In the hypothesized model for DPE samples, all observed variables are adequately explained with R-squared values ranging from 0.077 to 0.847. Latent variables are explained by their corresponding second order factors, ranging from 0.044 to 0.897.

Hypothesis testing using DPE samples

Overall, the structural model proposed (Model A) appeared to fit the sample data adequately, thus making it appropriate for hypothesis testing for DPE samples. Specifically, Hypothesis 1 was developed to examine the effect of employee perceptions on whether the adoption of HPWS was positively related to their job satisfaction. The results demonstrated a standardized coefficient of 0.525, SE = 0.045, $p < 0.001$. The positive relationship between these two variables was supported.

Hypothesis 2 assumes the positive relationship between employee perceptions on the adoption of HPWS and employee intention to stay in their current companies. The standardized coefficient of this path is 0.505, SE = 0.059, $p < 0.001$; therefore, the hypothesized relationship was supported.

Hypothesis 3 proposed that a relationship between employee perceptions of the adoption of HPWS are positively related to perceived trustworthiness. The results support this hypothesis with a standardized coefficient of 0.211, SE = 0.045, $p < 0.001$.

Hypothesis 4 postulated a positive relationship between employee perceptions of management's trustworthiness and job satisfaction. The result showed a standardized coefficient of 0.418, SE = 0.054, $p < 0.001$. The positive relation is confirmed.

Hypothesis 5 examined the positive relationship between employee perceptions of management's trustworthiness and the employee's turnover intention. The result demonstrated a standardized coefficient of 0.418, SE = 0.054, $p < 0.001$. This hypothesis is supported.

In order to investigate the mediating role of trustworthiness, bootstrapping was repeated. In the case of DPE samples, bias-corrected bootstrapping confidence intervals were obtained based on 5,000 bootstrap samples. The structural model indicated that the standardized indirect effect of trust on job satisfaction was 0.231, with bootstrapping 95 percent confidence intervals at 0.048 to 0.466. Zero was not contained in the confidence intervals, and the mediating relationship was ascertained. The same procedure was applied to assess the mediation between perceived HPWS and turnover intention. The standardized indirect effect of trust on turnover intention was 0.283, with 95 percent confidence intervals at 0.063 to 0.551. Zero was not contained in the confidence intervals, and the mediating relationship was supported.

Discussion

Understanding the underlying mechanisms of trust

Recognition of the importance of trust has grown considerately in recent years. Attempting to build trust between employees and employers is neither quick nor easy (Tyler and Degoey, 1995). This research models employee-perceived trust in

Table 5.9 Descriptive statistics and correlations for DPE samples

	SD	*Mean*	*1*	*2*	*3*	*4*	*5*	*6*	*7*	*8*	*9*	*10*
Staffing	1.045	0.000										
Internal mobility	1.600	0.000	0.324									
Performance	1.382	0.000	0.435	0.533								
Participation	1.512	0.000	0.398	0.489	0.656							
HPWS	0.538	0.000	0.514	0.630	0.846	0.776						
Ability	1.386	0.000	0.082	0.101	0.136	0.124	0.160					
Benevolence	1.154	0.000	0.094	0.116	0.155	0.142	0.183	0.661				
Integrity	1.279	0.000	0.103	0.126	0.169	0.155	0.200	0.720	0.823			
Trustworthiness	1.054	0.000	0.108	0.133	0.178	0.163	0.211	0.760	0.869	0.947		
Job Satisfaction	0.784	0.000	0.320	0.392	0.527	0.483	0.623	0.436	0.499	0.544	0.574	
Turnover Intention	1.126	0.000	0.305	0.374	0.502	0.460	0.593	0.399	0.456	0.497	0.525	0.964

Table 5.10 DPE model comparison

Model	*Substantive interpretation*	*Goodness of fit*		*Chi-square differences*			*RMSEA*	*CI*		*CFI*	*TLI*	*SRMR*	*AIC*
		$\chi2$	*df*	$\chi2$	*df*	*p* value		Lower	Higher				
A	Full model	1019.657	337				0.055	0.051	0.059	0.933	0.924	0.067	55531.647
B	Full model w/o JS–HPWS relationship	1150.272	338	130.615	1	3.006E-30	0.060	0.056	0.064	0.92	0.91	0.094	55688.455
C	Full model w/o TI–HPWS relationship	1084.763	338	65.106	1	7.098E-16	0.058	0.054	0.062	0.926	0.918	0.074	55608.514
D	Full model w/o Trust–HPWS relationship	1139.231	339	119.574	2	1.084E-26	0.060	0.056	0.064	0.921	0.912	0.098	55670.341
E	Full model w/o Trust–JS relationship	1134.779	338	115.122	1	7.4E-27	0.060	0.056	0.064	0.921	0.912	0.096	55667.623
F	Full model w/o Trust–TI relationship	1072.404	338	52.747	1	3.794E-13	0.057	0.053	0.061	0.928	0.919	0.078	55592.720

Note: JS: job satisfaction; TI: turnover intention.

their supervisors as a mediating factor on the relationship between perceived HPWS and employee outcomes. Mediation enables researchers to seek a more accurate explanation of the mechanisms that make a causal chain possible. In this investigation, a bootstrapping strategy was employed to test the mediation role of trust.

Development of trust consistently relies on the exchange paradigm (Blau, 1964; Luhmann and Schorr, 1979). Initially, the social exchange approach was developed with a focus on the development of trust between individuals. The application of social exchange theory assists in predicting how employees develop trust in managers. For example, if supervisors treat their subordinates favourably, such as adequately considering their viewpoints, suppressing their personal biases, applying decision-making criteria consistently, providing timely feedback after a decision and explaining their decision strongly (Tyler and Bies, 1990), employee trust in their supervisors is further reinforced. This trust-inducing process is consistent with the social exchange theory, which suggests that if employees receive favourable treatment from their supervisors, these employees may perceive an obligation to reciprocate with positive attitudes, including trust. In addition, the way supervisors treat employees suggests that they are worthy of that trust and do not take unfair advantage of their subordinates.

Nevertheless, employees are concerned about the fairness of procedures such as performance appraisals, which determine positive outcomes. The way managers implement such procedures is linked to the way employees perceive them and react to them. In this sense, managers and supervisors who are perceived positively when enacting work systems (such as performance appraisals) are likely to build trust in their subordinates.

With mutual trust between employees and their supervisors, it is expected that employees feel comfortable in dealing with people at work, believing their supervisors would communicate with them on critical issues and would not make decisions to jeopardize employees' positions. This potentially increases employee job satisfaction. Similarly, strong and positive bonds with supervisors lower the possibility of employees quitting.

Although the trusting environment in the workplace is not the object of this study, it is undeniable that a workplace with high levels of trust makes employees and managers build mutual trust more easily. As pointed out in the previous chapter, HPWS convey management expectations of their employees and determine how employees interpret HR policies and practices. It is possible that employees perceive employers who implement particular HPWS practices to be more trustworthy and prefer to work for these employers.

This research takes a step further towards developing and validating a multidimensional measurement of trustworthiness as perceived by employees in a work context. The selection of constructs was not random or arbitrary, and the study did not suggest the abandonment of the motivational lens. Rather, the measurement was based on scales adapted from previous research, which was established and validated in studies conducted in the West. A literature review and an EFA provide support for the construct validity. The measurement model suggests that each of the three dimensions contributes to an overall construct of trustworthiness in a second order factor analysis. The measurement was also informed by the interview findings. The interviewees revealed high expectations and reliance on management, as well as the effects of management on their own perceptions of HPWS and consequently their attitudes and behaviours at work.

Based on the bootstrapping results, the mediating effect of trust is confirmed. In addition, the model comparison further verified the existence of partial mediation rather than complete mediation. The supported mediating role of trust expands understanding of the underlying mechanism of HPWS. The recognition that all indirect effects are partial may serve as a cue that other mediators can be considered (Shrout and Bolger, 2002).

HPWS and employee job satisfaction and intention to stay

Besides the partial mediation role of trust, statistical results established a direct relationship between HPWS and employee job satisfaction and employee minimal intention of leaving. In contrast to studies which used data collected from the West, this study tested the positive effect of HPWS on employee outcomes using samples in SOEs and DPEs in China. Both types of enterprises are considered to be Chinese indigenous; in other words, they are expected to demonstrate more Chinese characteristics in comparison with joint ventures (JVs) and foreign invested enterprises (FIEs) in China.

Creating and retaining valuable human capital for sustained competitive advantage is important for business success. Exploration on enhancing employee job satisfaction and lowering intentions to leave is therefore meaningful and helpful to management as a method of increasing the possibility of retaining valuable employees. It also indicates a possible way of influencing employees in order to motivate and keep them.

HPWS in SOEs and in DPEs

Despite an insufficient empirical support of HPWS in the context of China, the current study made an effort to identify the HR policies and practices within HPWS which have been adopted in SOEs and DPEs. A comparison of HPWS in SOEs and DPEs has helped answer a key question of this research about similarities and differences between these two types of enterprises.

The constructs of HPWS have been selected and identified in factor analysis. EFA results indicate that the HR dimensions with significant loadings are similar between SOEs and DPEs; however, these HR dimensions/functions, including staffing, internal mobility, performance management and participation, were valued differently by employees. In the current study, HPWS has been treated as an integrated concept. The difference between detailed individual HR practices will be discussed in the next chapter, where the results of two studies are combined.

Conclusion

This chapter has presented the findings from the surveys in the second stage of this research. SEM was employed to process the data in an exploratory and then confirmatory manner. The data analysis process commenced with data screening to ensure the underlying assumptions pertaining to normality, missing values and outliers were supported. Exploratory factor analysis was then performed because the measurement model was not extensively tested in China. This procedure is considered important and necessary in testing and developing theory. Confirmatory factor analyses were then performed on the measurement models related to perceived HPWS, perceived trustworthiness, job satisfaction and intention to stay. The results confirmed the construct reliability and validity. After the measurement models were determined to be satisfactory, the structural model proposed to explore HPWS implementation. The mediating effect of trust was tested using a bootstrapping strategy. The hypothesized path relationships as outlined in chapter 2 were mostly corroborated by the structural model.

In summary, this chapter has presented the results of the quantitative study (Stage Two study) which intends to test the findings statistically across a larger number of samples. The results confirmed the partial mediation role of trust as a positive linkage between HPWS and job satisfaction and intention to stay. It also verifies the direct effect of HPWS on these employee outcomes using data collected from Chinese indigenous enterprises. Given that HPWS are not implemented in a vacuum and are influenced by many factors, the variations of HPWS in terms of motives, understanding, designs and implementation may lead to different employee perceptions and responses. Detailed discussion will be presented in the next chapter, incorporating findings from both qualitative and quantitative studies.

References

Anderson, J. C. and Gerbing, D. W. 1988. Structural equation modeling in practice: A review and recommended two-step approach. *Psychological Bulletin*, 103, 411–423.

Barrett, P. 2007. Structural equation modelling: Adjudging model fit. *Personality and Individual Differences*, 42, 815–824.

Behling, O. and Law, K. S. 2000. *Translating questionnaires and other research instruments: Problems and solutions*, London: Sage.

Beltrán-Martín, I., Roca-Puig, V., Escrig-Tena, A. and Bou-Llusar, J. C. 2008. Human resource flexibility as a mediating variable between high performance work systems and performance. *Journal of Management*, 34, 1009–1044.

Bentler, P. M. 1978. The interdependence of theory, methodology, and empirical data: Causal modeling as an approach to construct validation. In: Kandel, D. B. (ed.), *Longitudinal Drug Research*. New York: Wiley.

Blau, P. M. 1964. *Exchange and power in social life*, Piscataway, NJ: Transaction Publishers.

Boomsma, A. 2000. Reporting analyses of covariance structures. *Structural Equation Modeling*, 7, 461–483.

Brown, T. 2006. CFA with equality constraints, multiple groups, and mean structures. In: Kenny, D.A. (ed.), *Confirmatory Factor Analysis for Applied Research*. New York: Guilford Press.

Byrne, B. M. 2012. *A primer of LISREL: Basic applications and programming for confirmatory factor analytic models*, New York, NY: Springer Science & Business Media.

Campbell, D. T. 1960. Blind variation and selective retentions in creative thought as in other knowledge processes. *Psychological Review*, 67, 380–400.
Campbell, D. T. and Fiske, D. W. 1959. Convergent and discriminant validation by the multitrait-multimethod matrix. *Psychological Bulletin*, 56, 81–105.
Chou, C.-P. and Bentler, P. M. 1995. Estimates and tests in structural equation modeling. In: Hoyle, R. H. (ed.) *Structural Equation Modeling: Concepts, Issues, and Applications*. Thousand Oaks, CA: Sage.
Cohen, J., Cohen, P., West, S. G. and Aiken, L. S. 2013. *Applied multiple regression/correlation analysis for the behavioral sciences*, Abingdon: Routledge.
Diamantopoulos, A., Siguaw, J. A. and Siguaw, J. A. 2000. *Introducing LISREL: A guide for the uninitiated*, London: Sage.
Fabrigar, L. R., Wegener, D. T., Maccallum, R. C., Strahan, E. J. and Appelbaum, M. I. 1999. Evaluating the use of exploratory factor analysis in psychological research. *Psychological Methods*, 4, 272–299.
Gorsuch, R. L. and Hao, J. Y. 1993. Forgiveness: An exploratory factor analysis and its relationships to religious variables. *Review of Religious Research*, 34, 333–347.
Hackman, J. R. and Oldham, G. R. 1980. *Work redesign*. Reading, MA: Addison-Wesley.
Hair, J. F. 1998. *Multivariate data analysis*, Upper Saddle River, NJ: Prentice Hall.
Hall, R. J., Snell, A. F. and Foust, M. S. 1999. Item parceling strategies in SEM: Investigating the subtle effects of unmodeled secondary constructs. *Organizational Research Methods*, 2, 233–256.
Hayduk, L. A. and Glaser, D. N. 2000. Jiving the four-step, waltzing around factor analysis, and other serious fun. *Structural Equation Modeling*, 7, 1–35.
Hu, L. T. and Bentler, P. M. 1999. Cutoff criteria for fit indexes in covariance structure analysis: Conventional criteria versus new alternatives. *Structural Equation Modeling: A Multidisciplinary Journal*, 6, 1–55.
Irving, P. G., Coleman, D. F. and Cooper, C. L. 1997. Further assessments of a three-component model of occupational commitment: Generalizability and differences across occupations. *Journal of Applied Psychology*, 82, 444.
Kline, R. B. 2005. *Principles and practice of structural equation modeling*, New York, NY: Guilford.
Kocabasoglu, C., Prahinski, C. and Klassen, R. D. 2007. Linking forward and reverse supply chain investments: The role of business uncertainty. *Journal of Operations Management*, 25, 1141–1160.
Law, K. S., Wong, C.-S. and Mobley, W. M. 1998. Toward a taxonomy of multidimensional constructs. *Academy of Management Review*, 23, 741–755.
Luhmann, N. and Schorr, K. E. 1979. *Reflexionsprobleme im Erziehungssystem*. Stuttgart: Klett-Cotta.
Mackinnon, D. P., Lockwood, C. M., Hoffman, J. M., West, S. G. and Sheets, V. 2002. A comparison of methods to test mediation and other intervening variable effects. *Psychological Methods*, 7, 83–104.
Mayer, R. C. and Davis, J. H. 1999. The effect of the performance appraisal system on trust for management: A field quasi-experiment. *Journal of Applied Psychology*, 84, 123.
Mcdonald, R. P. and Ho, M.-H. R. 2002. Principles and practice in reporting structural equation analyses. *Psychological Methods*, 7, 64–82.
Podsakoff, P. M., Mackenzie, S. B., Lee, J.-Y. and Podsakoff, N. P. 2003. Common method biases in behavioral research: A critical review of the literature and recommended remedies. *Journal of Applied Psychology*, 88, 879–903.

Raykov, T. and Shrout, P. E. 2002. Reliability of scales with general structure: Point and interval estimation using a structural equation modeling approach. *Structural Equation Modeling*, 9, 195–212.

Shrout, P. E. and Bolger, N. 2002. Mediation in experimental and nonexperimental studies: New procedures and recommendations. *Psychological Methods*, 7, 422–445.

Stevens, J. P. 2012. *Applied multivariate statistics for the social sciences*, Abingdon: Routledge.

Sun, L.-Y., Aryee, S. and Law, K. S. 2007. High-performance human resource practices, citizenship behavior, and organizational performance: A relational perspective. *Academy of Management Journal*, 50, 558–577.

Tabachnick, B. and Fidell, L. 2007. Multivariate analysis of variance and covariance. *Using Multivariate Statistics*, 3, 402–407.

Thompson, B. and Daniel, L. G. 1996. Factor analytic evidence for the construct validity of scores: A historical overview and some guidelines. *Educational and Psychological Measurement*, 56, 197–208.

Tyler, T. R. and Bies, R. J. 1990. Beyond formal procedures: The interpersonal context of procedural justice. *Applied Social Psychology and Organizational Settings*, 77, 98–117.

Tyler, T. R. and Degoey, P. 1995. Collective restraint in social dilemmas: Procedural justice and social identification effects on support for authorities. *Journal of Personality and Social Psychology*, 69, 482–497.

Ullman, S. E., Townsend, S. M., Filipas, H. H. and Starzynski, L. L. 2007. Structural models of the relations of assault severity, social support, avoidance coping, self-blame, and PTST among sexual assault survivors. *Psychology of Women Quarterly*, 31, 23–37.

Yuan, K.-H. and Bentler, P. M. 2004. On chi-square difference and z tests in mean and covariance structure analysis when the base model is misspecified. *Educational and Psychological Measurement*, 64, 737–757.

6 Conclusion

On-going challenges

Introduction

In recent years, concerns for the sustainability of China's exponential economic growth have been raised. Global expansion has increased competition while economic reforms have amplified privatizations of SOEs and the introduction and expansion of DPEs. These public and private domestic companies are now competing in the same arena albeit under different constraints. SOEs are controlled by government policy while DPEs are more flexible as they do not have the same restrictions. How might organizations in China adopt and modify existing Western HRM systems in order to enhance their competitiveness? Generally management's perspective is usually considered, with less attention being paid to the perspective of employees. This discrepancy is the central concern of this book.

SHRM is an established method used by organizations to shape human resources to fit pre-established organizational plans (Leopold et al., 2005); most notable is the managerial perspective. Yet competitive advantage comes from the expertise and skills of individual managers along with those of employees (Barney, 1991). The way managers implement human resources systems influences the way that employees perceive these systems. Managers who adopt HPWS in the West enhance positive employee attitudes and improve retention. However, questions arise as to how indigenous companies in China may best achieve positive outcomes. In response, we address four questions based on the research carried out in this book:

- What are the SHRM/HPWS adopted and implemented in China from manager and employee perspectives?
- What insights can we gain about SHRM and HPWS in SOEs and DPEs in China?
- What HRM systems can organizations develop to encourage positive attitudes and intentions to stay?
- What direction should managers and organizations take in implementing strategies for HRM and HPWS?

The key objective of this book is to explore the adoption and implementation of SHRM in general, and HPWS in particular, in SOEs and DPEs. This study also aims to develop a better understanding of how SHRM/HPWS influence employees in terms of their job satisfaction and turnover intention.

Managers' perspectives – adoption and implementation of SHRM

In order to respond quickly to fierce competition, Chinese enterprises have increased their adoption of Western HR practices (Warner, 2004). According to the managers who were interviewed, SHRM policies and practices are extensively adopted and implemented in the areas of staffing, training, rewarding, performance management and employee participation.

According to managers, every effort is made to align staffing policies and practices in SOEs and DPEs with business strategy. In particular, DPEs need to quickly adopt staffing policies and practice business strategies which will enable them to pre-empt external market volatility and skills shortages. Adopting new staffing policies and practices in SOEs is less feasible. First, SOEs are regulated by local or national governments, which prioritize long-term development rather than short-term gain, affecting business strategies and staffing policies and practices. In addition, the structure and employment quota system is strictly regulated, which limits staffing fluctuations. Furthermore, stable, longer term employment compared to that of their private counterparts leads to a static workforce.

Alternately, the dynamic environment requires that in order for DPEs to remain competitive they must allocate all resources, including human resources, efficiently. DPEs need to react quickly and adjust staffing policies and practices to reflect environmental changes and meet business demand. Flexibility is achieved by short-term position offers which lead to high employee turnover. Nonetheless, large size DPEs are beginning to view staffing from a long-term perspective. Overall, traditional staffing practices are more prevalent in SOEs than DPEs. For example, interviews with prospective employees take precedence over selection tests in SOEs, whereas DPEs favour selection tests over interviews. DPEs also use personal competencies as a major selection criterion, whereas SOEs additionally emphasize academic qualifications and political background.

The common practice of staffing using referrals by friends and relatives which increase chances of selection is consistent in both SOEs and DPEs. Generally, SOEs are more attractive to employees due to the offer of longer term tenures and clear career development paths. DPEs, especially small size or newly established companies, face challenges in finding suitable employees due to less job security and their unstable financial position. Referrals from friends and relatives provide DPEs with an alternative source for recruiting potential employees.

Managers interviewed commented on training policies and practices in SOEs and DPEs. In most cases these areas concern generic training such as orientation training or 'pre-post training' for new employees to become familiar with the company's culture, history, structure and policies. SOEs are regulated by the government and are required to have training budgets approved, to comply with on-the-job training and increasingly to comply with off-the-job training.

Off-the-job training in SOEs includes but is not limited to attending local colleges or training centres, lectures and distance learning. Financial assistance from the government enhances employee training opportunities as well as monetary support for employees to pursue work-related qualifications outside their workplace.

DPEs, on the other hand, generally have limited training budgets to provide employees with on-the-job training, which includes online training, mentoring, apprenticeships and understudies. Small DPEs provide the minimum amount of training required. Yet, as DPEs grow in size, managers consider the longer term development of employees and establish in-house training systems. A well-designed and customized training system increases employee–employer fit as well as contributes to employee self-esteem, which enhances satisfaction with and commitment to the company. Small DPEs only provide basic and minimum training. Nevertheless, for the majority of DPEs, training is considered to be a cost, and return on investment is a much discussed issue, especially when employees leave before the organization has time to recoup costs.

Managers also commented on performance management, which differed between SOEs and DPEs. The performance management policies and practices of DPEs were closely tied to their business strategy, in contrast to SOE policies and practices which reflected the business strategy to a lesser degree. In order for DPEs to survive and obtain sustained competitive advantage in the dynamic marketplace, flexibility and a quick response to market changes and market demand are necessary. Performance management policies and practices reflect managerial expectations which change with business strategy and lead to a frequent and continuous revision. DPEs assess employee performance frequently in order to achieve business strategies. Larger DPEs continuously optimize employee skills compositions to realize their business strategies.

Performance management policies and practices for SOEs do not reflect the external environment and are a less important link to business strategy. Strategies in SOEs are normally for the long-term and remain relatively stable over time. Simultaneously, the performance management systems remain constant. SOEs mainly rely on objective assessment criteria such as absenteeism, which precludes the assessment of employee performance. Yet assessing employee performance is fraught with problems. Although the relationship between colleagues and supervisors in China is critical, it adds to the difficulty of providing impartial colleague or supervisor performance assessment. Employees tend to overrate these performances when they have a close relationship with particular people. SOEs also rely on inefficient performance management as job security precludes job loss regardless of unsatisfactory performance.

Managers interviewed also discussed reward systems. Since SOEs are government owned, they are also funded by government and depend on the budget, which has been predetermined at the beginning of a financial year. Therefore, employee wage calculations are made using specific formulas provided by the government. Employee wages are relatively fixed across sectors, and pay rates for employees are fairly stable. In contrast to SOEs, employee wages in DPEs vary significantly between companies. Employee wages in DPEs are determined by senior management at a level higher than the minimum wage. Additionally, the wages can be adjusted on a continuous basis to reflect the shifting focus of business development as well as revenue and profit margin.

Rewards such as bonuses and benefits are allocated according to different criteria in SOEs and DPEs. The intention of bonuses is to recognize high achievement and to improve performance. Managers in SOEs emphasize collective effort and teamwork and consequently distribute bonuses based on team performance, while DPEs award bonuses based on individual performance. Rewards in SOEs in the form of employee benefit schemes (e.g., share ownership and other monetary as well as non-monetary rewards such as free meals and transport, holidays and in-kind gifts) are few and loosely managed, while the situation is the opposite in DPEs. The difference is attributed to differences in ownership. Privately owned firms such as DPEs, which operate in dynamic environments, have difficulty retaining valuable employees who are enticed elsewhere by benefits offered by other firms. One strong incentive to stay is the benefit of share ownership, which turns employees into 'owners' of the enterprise. Bonuses and benefits are expressions of managerial expectations of employee attitudes and behaviours. These rewards encourage and reinforce employee attitude and behaviour and achieve the objectives of the business strategy.

A final topic discussed by managers in the interviews was the issue of promotion within the context of the three types of companies considered – namely, SOEs, large DPEs and small DPEs. Career paths and promotion availability in both SOEs and large DPEs are explicit. Employees in SOEs are promoted based on their seniority, professional titles, academic qualifications and age. This basis for promotion ensures the smooth and stable operation of SOEs to the detriment of adaptability to change. Long-term sustained development is a shared feature between SOEs and larger DPEs. Consequently, larger DPEs provide clear career pathways but also optimize resources and provide flexibility by offering employees career path choices. Unlike SOEs and larger DPEs, smaller DPEs are constrained by resources, such as capital and staff members. Promotion in smaller DPEs is controlled by senior managers or the business owner. Decisions on promotion rest on factors such as social connection, emotional factors, company needs and profession. Generally speaking, strong social connections and emotional factors (e.g., trust in supervisor and sense of belonging) are likely to strengthen the employee–manager relationship and pre-empt a promotion.

Employees' perspectives – awareness of SHRM implementation

The previous section presented the similarities and differences between SOEs and DPEs on the adoption and implementation of SHRM and relevant issues from management perspectives. This section discusses the issues from the employee perspective.

When asked about the organization's staffing practices, employees who were interviewed were concerned with a number of issues. Fairness of the selection process caused the most unease. Friend and relative referrals were a major issue as these referrals could create unequal opportunities among employees in the future. Employees' development may be hampered and promotion may be hindered as the possibility of selection from a large pool of job applicants shrinks. Employees also felt that these referrals would have an impact on employers in terms of overlooking their capabilities and contributions. In both SOEs and DPEs employees felt strongly about the benefits their firms provided: the job security provided by SOEs and the ability to develop quickly and the offer of generous employee benefit schemes by the larger DPEs. Consequently, the issue of fairness is not one to be overlooked. As social exchange theory suggests, employees may work inefficiently as a response to not being valued and cared for by supervisors/managers.

Employees interviewed perceived training as an investment by the company towards their well-being – a way by which employees can be made to feel valued. Employees in both SOEs and DPEs are selected to attend certain training programs, which are considered a form of reward. Training is perceived positively by employees and contributes to their positive attitudes and retention. Off-the-job training is preferred by SOEs while DPEs favour on-the-job training and vocational education to accommodate employee skills needs. Employees observe and form perceptions about the selections made by their supervisors or managers of the employees who should receive training. The attitude of employees towards their superiors and their decision to stay or leave is especially important in DPEs based on whether their superiors provide the training needed by employees, whether superiors can select the most qualified employees for further training and whether they can encourage 'low performers' to perform better after training. In SOEs and DPEs high performers receive further special training, which leads to even better performance. Recognition of these high performers creates a feeling of accomplishment, which potentially increases employee commitment and job satisfaction.

Performance management is related to training and rewarding, both of which are treated seriously by employees. The interviews and the survey suggest that employees are aware of performance management policies and practices since performance management is closely correlated to employee wages, which in turn affect employees' quality of life, motivating them to gain information about these HR practices. Another factor relates to the employees who are proactively involved in the performance management process (as the employee interviews suggest). These employees approach their supervisors/managers for detailed information and discuss relevant issues that might influence their performance outcome. Extensive participation increases employees' awareness of performance management policies and practices. In addition, there are differences between performance management implementation in DPEs and SOEs. Employees interviewed believed that DPE managers were more accessible and adaptable than managers in SOEs. For example, SOE employees were de-motivated by wages that were not calculated based on performance.

Employees stated that rewards provide them with a strong incentive to align their own goals with the organization's business targets. In general, employee attitudes and behaviour favoured by managers are encouraged and reinforced by a reward system. Generous reward policies and practices encourage employees to work hard and to stay longer in the organization. Employees stated that benefit packages range from work-related to life-related benefits, such as project bonuses, free meals, free transportation and free accommodation. Employee experience of rewards ranged from share ownership schemes to match-making for a possible marriage. Regardless of the form of employee reward, employee benefit packages offered outside the working environment signal to employees that they are valued and that they can be part of the big 'family' and be taken care of. According to the employee interviews, reward practices in DPEs are superior to those in SOEs, and DPEs are able to provide employees with extra rewards which match their performance.

Similar to employees' concerns about other HR functions, fair distribution based on an equitable rewarding system is critical. Employees in our sample prefer differential reward allocation based on their contribution rather than equal allocations for a similar pay. Equal pay allocation appears to de-motivate employees because higher performers and lower performers are rewarded in the same way, thus discouraging efforts to achieve a better outcome. Additionally, equal allocation makes employees feel that their managers are indifferent to their contributions or that their managers are incapable of using rewards effectively, both of which deteriorate employees' commitment towards the company and their trust in their supervisors/managers.

As younger workers in China are becoming more educated, they are increasingly aware of the expectations they have of their employment relationship (Zhu et al., 2014). The advantage is that the younger generation of employees is more likely to enter an employment relationship with a clear idea of what is expected of them and what they want to gain. The fulfilment of employees' expectations gives them motivation to perform better and stay with their current employer longer. However, a disadvantage is that, if employees' expectations are not met, their commitment to an organization is likely to decline.

In summary, employees can be affected by SHRM policies and practices in at least two ways. Employees form perceptions of HR practices as these practices signal managerial expectations. Additionally, managers adopt SHRM policies and practices, such as generous employee benefits, in order to encourage and reinforce employees' positive attitudes and behaviours at work. This positive relationship is supported by the employee survey performed in this study (i.e., the second, statistics-gathering stage). The survey illustrated that perceptions of SHRM/HPWS were positively associated with job satisfaction in SOEs and DPEs (see the detailed results in chapter 5) as well as with employees' intention of staying in both SOEs and DPEs.

Reflections

Studying SHRM/HPW systems that have developed in the West and have been introduced in another country such as China is thought provoking. This book is among the first to shed light on our understanding of how SHRM/HPWS influence employee attitudes and intentions in China. Moreover, this book provides insights beyond a Chinese and Western model. In the following we reflect on some of the important aspects of our research in the Chinese context.

One key reflection concerns the contextual differences between the indigenous companies (SOEs and DPEs) which affect SHRM. Even though SHRM policies and practices in SOEs and DPEs are aligned with business strategies, the context affects the speed with which SHRM can be changed. Flexibility is hampered in SOEs by long-term contracts, hierarchy and traditional norms. SOEs have long-term business strategies which reflect relatively stable HR policies and practices, whereas DPEs have shorter-term business strategies which continuously adjust HR policies and practices in order to maintain competitiveness.

Although there is no agreement about the composition of HPWS, most mainstream Western literature claims one key element, namely participation, to be an important component (Appelbaum, 2000; Macky and Boxall, 2008; Lawler III, 1986). With the introduction a new Labour Contract Law in 2008, greater employee rights and participative labour relations were emphasized. This feature is also highlighted in our fieldwork, although it was found that employee participation was limited. Improved commitment to work was evident when managers realized the importance of involving employees in the adoption of SHRM policies and practices and included them in the decision-making process.

Interviewees also considered traditional Chinese culture and the organization's own culture to impact on SHRM/HPWS. HR practices are more or less culture sensitive (Evans and Lorange, 1989). Employees weighted interpersonal relationships heavily. They were reluctant to confront their managers or colleagues about issues at work, which slowed knowledge transfer and addressing performance management issues. The avoidance of confrontation also decelerated the implementation of HPWS in the working environment. Although employees were free to communicate with managers and voice their opinions in the working environment, this was the case only sporadically and not continually. Employee participation in decision-making was therefore limited.

Generational differences were also evident as issues among the managers and employees we interviewed. These differences meant that different age groups had different characteristics and responses to SHRM/HPWS. The younger the employees, the greater their flexibility and mobility, making retention difficult. Employees who were in their early 20s were risk-takers, looking for challenges, fun and high paying jobs, and were quick to adapt to changes in the working environment, including changes in HR policies and practices. Older employees in their 30s were easier to retain as they wanted greater stability and planning in their career. They were ready to compromise and balance their interests with those of their employer. In comparison with other age groups, their participation is spontaneous, which exposes them to more influences from HR policies and practices. The oldest employees were in their 40s. Generally, this group is experienced and skilled, but may not work as hard as younger employees. Unless their interests are significantly jeopardized, they prefer to remain passive.

One other key reflection concerns the difference between manager and employee perspectives of HRM. Managers focus on organizational macro issues such as efficiency, productivity and financial status and often ignore employee concerns. This gap directly affects employee levels of job satisfaction and turnover intention. Hence, if employees interpret managerial expectations as they were intended and respond accordingly, they are likely to be rewarded for their performance, thus enhancing their job satisfaction and commitment, which is likely to minimize withdrawal intentions. This is in line with Western literature (Guest et al., 2003). The way employees perceive HRM practices also indirectly affects these positive outcomes through feelings of trust. When employees are treated favourably as a result of fulfilling employer expectations, trust between them is reinforced. According to social exchange theory (Blau, 1964), if employees receive favourable treatment from their supervisors, employees may perceive an obligation to reciprocate with positive attitudes, including trust. Trust can only be built through the clarity of interpersonal communication (Bambacas and Patrickson, 2008).

Practical implications

From a practical perspective, implications from our fieldwork extend beyond Chinese organizations and those in the West to the global setting. Organizations across countries have utilized and found the positive effects of SHRM (Chen and Huang, 2009; Chuang and Liao, 2010) as well as HPWS (Demirbag et al., 2015). Arguably, the goal for management in implementing SHRM/HPWS is to evoke several positive outcomes, especially performance outcomes. The critical question is how to achieve these objectives. A key challenge is ensuring HR policies and practices are enacted consistently by employees across the organization. How HR policies and practices are implemented and in turn interpreted by employees critically affects their attitudes (e.g., job satisfaction) and intentions of staying or leaving. Therefore, there is a need for management to move beyond a focus on the effective design or selection of a HR system to include an emphasis on the way these HR policies and practices are communicated.

The results of this study indicate that employee perceptions of SHRM/HPWS are likely to affect their level of attitudinal and behavioural outcomes. In particular, the HR practices that managers adopt and the way these are implemented signals to employees the organization's intentions. Findings from this study suggest that communication between employees and managers is imperative. Literature asserts that the clarity of the message managers send and their leadership style influences employee attitudes, yet it is this skill of being able to clearly relay a message that is most lacking in managers (Bambacas and Patrickson, 2008).

Furthermore, research findings indicate that a new management system is required for the changing expectations of the new style of employee in China. Another generation of employees has different expectations from that of employees in the past. Changing government policies about treatment of employees have encouraged employees' expectations of their employers. Coupled with the dynamic and competitive environment, China finds itself at a cross-roads. Implementing SHRM/HPWS is becoming crucial. Our fieldwork suggests that the quality of HR systems is likely to have a positive outcome for organizations. The continual revision of HR systems according to the competitive external environment seems to be a given for organizations in China. In order to gain and maintain competitiveness in the global arena, China needs to move from the 'Made in China' mind-set to that of 'Create in China'. This is a start, but this book also illustrates that China still has a long way to go.

Concluding remarks

This book contributes to the debates on the adoption and implementation of SHRM/HPWS in a non-Western country, namely China, by using case studies of indigenous SOEs and DPEs. Although this research focuses on the case studies of Chinese companies, the implications reach beyond China. In any indigenous company, in any transitional economy under the influence of globalization, management are required to effectively utilize their human resources; employees are increasingly aware of their rights and are actively (or willingly) involved in key decision-making processes that fundamentally influence their working and family lives. This book has provided a detailed analysis of a number of important areas in this regard. Hopefully, the eventual outcomes of this effort may generate some meaningful changes in the areas of SHRM/HPWS in non-Western societies, both theoretically and practically.

References

Appelbaum, E. 2000. *Manufacturing advantage: Why high-performance work systems pay off*, Ithaca, NY: Cornell University Press.

Bambacas, M. and Patrickson, M. 2008. Interpersonal communication skills that enhance organisational commitment. *Journal of Communication Management*, 12, 51–72.

Barney, J. B. 1991. Firm resource-based theories of competitive advantage. *Journal of Management*, 17, 99–120.

Blau, P. M. 1964. *Exchange and power in social life*, New York: John Wiley & Sons.

Chen, C.-J. and Huang, J.-W. 2009. Strategic human resource practices and innovation performance – The mediating role of knowledge management capacity. *Journal of Business Research*, 62, 104–114.

Chuang, C.-H. and Liao, H. 2010. Strategic human resource management in service context: Taking care of business by taking care of employees and customers. *Personnel Psychology*, 63, 153–196.

Demirbag, M., Tatoglu, E. and Wilkinson, A. 2015. Adoption of high-performance work systems by local subsidiaries of developed country and Turkish MNEs and indigenous firms in Turkey. *Human Resource Management* [Online]. Available: http://dx.doi.org/10.1002/hrm.21706 [Online early].

Evans, P. and Lorange, P. 1989. The two logics behind human resource management. In: Evans, P., Doz, Y. and Laurent, A. (ed.) *Human Resource Management in International Firms: Change, Globalization, Innovation*. London: Macmillan.

Guest, D. E., Michie, J., Conway, N. and Sheehan, M. 2003. Human resource management and corporate performance in the UK. *British Journal of Industrial Relations*, 41, 291–314.

Lawler III, E. E. 1986. *High-involvement management*. San Francisco: Jossey-Bass.

Leopold, J., Harris, L. and Watson, T. 2005. Employee participation, involvement, and communications. *The Strategic Managing of Human Resource*. Essex, UK: Prentice-Hall Pearson Education.

Macky, K. and Boxall, P. 2008. High-involvement work processes, work intensification and employee well-being: A study of New Zealand worker experiences. *Asia Pacific Journal of Human Resources*, 46, 38–55.

Warner, M. 2004. Human resource management in China revisited: Introduction. *The International Journal of Human Resource Management*, 15, 617–634.

Zhu, Y., Xie, Y., Warner, M. and Guo, Y. 2014. Employee participation and the influence on job satisfaction of the 'new generation' of Chinese employees. *The International Journal of Human Resource Management*, 26(19), 2395–2411.

Appendix 1: Interview questions for managers

Introduction

This interview is constructed in order to explore the adoption and implementation of SHRM/HPWS in China. It will assist us to analyse current situation of SHRM/HPWS in China and understand its impact on organizational and individual performance.

It is divided into three main parts.

1. The first part asks for general information about you and your organization.
2. The second part asks about specific SHRM/HPWS policy and practices in your organization.
3. The third part asks about external and internal environmental factors that might affect your organization's performance.

Please answer each question and add any comments if you would like to. All responses are held in strictest confidence. We appreciate and thank you for your participation.

General Information:

Name of Company

____

Address

____

Industry Sector

____

Ownership of Company

____

Size of Company

____

Current Position ____________________ Gender____________________

Highest education level achieved____________________________________

Date of Interview_________________

Beginning time __________________ Finishing time_________________

1 Recruiting and Selecting

1.1 What are the strategic goals for recruiting and selecting employees in your organization?

____

____

1.2 During the process of recruiting and selecting, how do you realise these strategic goals? Please provide examples.

____

____

1.3 What impact, do you expect, these recruiting and selecting practices have on current and potential employees?

____

____

1.4 Do you intend to make any changes to the recruiting and selecting practices in your organization? Why? What changes will you make?

____

____

2 Performance Management

2.1 What are the strategic goals for managing employees' performance in your organization?

____

____

2.2 What are the criteria you set for performance at the different management levels?

Top-Level Managers ____

Middle-LevelManagers_______________________________________

First-Level Managers (i.e. line managers or supervisors) _____________

Non-managerial staff:

Professional and administrative workers__________________________

Manual Workers____

2.3 How do you implement the performance standards, in order to achieve your strategic goals? Please provide examples.

____

____

2.4 What impact do these performance standards you set have on your employees?

____

____

2.5 What changes do you intend to make for improving current performance management system in your organization? Please explain.

____

____

3 Employee Development and Training

3.1 What are the strategic goals for employees' training in your organization?

____

____

3.2 How do you achieve your strategic goals with the employee training practices? Please provide examples.

____

____

3.3 What impact do these training practices have on your employees?

____

____

3.4 What changes do you intend to make to current training practices in your organization?

____

____

4 Promotion and Career Management

4.1 What are the strategic goals for managing employees' promotion and career development in your organization?

____

____

4.2 How do you achieve your strategic goals by managing your employees' career? Please provide examples.

____

____

4.3 What impact do these career practices have on employees?

____

____

4.4 Do you intend to make any changes to the current promotion and career management system in your organization? What do you intend doing? Please explain.

____

____

5 Rewarding

5.1 What are the strategic goals for rewarding employees in your organization?

____

____

5.2 How do you achieve your strategic goals by rewarding your employees? Please provide examples.

____

____

5.3 What are key components of salary package in your organization? For different positions

Top-Level Managers ______________________________

Middle-Level Managers ______________________________

First-Level Managers (i.e. line managers or supervisors) ______________

Non-managerial staff:

Professional and administrative workers ______________________

Manual Workers ______________________________

5.4 Are there any other benefit programs provided to your employees?

____

____

5.5 What impact do these systems have on your employees?

____

____

5.6 What changes do you intend to make to the current reward system in your organization? Please explain.

____

____

6 Employees' retention

6.1 What retention policies and practices do you have for employees at different level?

____

____

6.2 What impact do these retention policies and practices have on your employees?

____

____

6.3 Do you intend to make any changes to your current retention policies and practices in your organization?

____

____

7 Overall Employees' involvement

7.1 In which way are your employees involved in each HR activity in your organization?

____

____

7.2 What impact, do you think, these employees' involvement practices have on your employees?

____

____

7.3 Do you intend to make changes to the involvement employees have with the HR practices in your organization? Why? Please explain.

____

____

8 Organizational performance

By adopting strategic human resource management system in your organization, how much does organizational performance improve?

Changes in productivity______________________________

Efficiency (hourly performance) ________________________

Skillperformance____________________________________

Turnover rate_______________________________________

9 External environment Analysis

Please provide example(s) about how the following factors influence strategic human resource management in your organizations (e.g. government policy, labour laws and regulation, unemployment, and technology development).

____

____

____

____

10 Internal environment analysis

Please provide example(s) about how the following factors influence strategic human resource management in your organization (e.g. organizational culture, company structure, organizational norms, and union).

____

____

____

____

11 Future challenges

Given the radical changes in market and within organization, how will strategic human resource management system in your organization cope with these changes in future?

____

____

____

____

Appendix 2: Interview Questions for Employees

Introduction

This interview is constructed in order to explore the adoption and implementation of SHRM/HPWS in China. It will assist us to analyse current situation of SHRM/HPWS in China and understand its impact on organizational and individual performance.

This interview is divided into two main parts.

4 The first part asks for general information about you and your organization.
5 The second part asks about specific SHRM/HPWS policy and practices in your organization.

Please answer each question and add any comments if you would like to. All responses are held in strictest confidence. We appreciate and thank you for your participation.

General Information:

Name of Company

____

Address ____

Industry Sector

____

Ownership of Company

____

Size of Company

____

Current Position __________________ Gender__________________

Seniority (Years)______________________________________

Highest education level achieved___________________________

Date of Interview ____________________

Beginning time ____________________ Finishing time____________________

1 Recruiting and Selecting

1.1 What is your view on recruiting and selecting practices in your organization?

____

____

1.2 What impact do the recruiting and selecting practices have on you?

____

____

1.3 What suggestions will you make to current recruiting and selecting practices in your organization?

____

____

2 Performance Management

2.1 What is your view on performance system in your organization?

____

____

2.2 What impact do the performance management have on you?

____

____

2.3 What suggestions will you make for improving current performance management system in your organization?

____

____

3 Employee Development and Training

3.1 What is your view on training practices in your organization?

____

____

3.2 What impact do these training practices have on you?

____

____

3.3 What suggestions do you intend to make for training practices in your organization?

____

____

4 Promotion and Career Management

4.1 How do promotion and career development practices in your organization help you manage your career goals?

___

___

4.2 What is your view on current promotion and career development practices?

___

___

4.3 Do you intend to make any suggestions on current promotion and career management system in your organization? What suggestions will you make?

___

___

5 Rewarding

5.1 What is your view on current rewarding practices in your organization?

___

___

5.2 What impact do these rewarding practices have on you?

___

___

5.3 What suggestions will you make for improving current rewarding practices in your organization?

___

___

6 Employees' retention

6.1 What is your view on retention policies and practices in your organization?

___

___

6.2 What impact do these policies and practices have on you?

___

___

6.3 What suggestion do you intend to make for improving employees' retention policies in your organization?

___

___

7 **Overall Employees' involvement**

7.1 What are the practices for involving employees in your organizations?

____

____

7.2 In which ways are you involved in each human resource activity in your organization?

Recruiting and Selecting____________________________

Performance Management____________________________

Employee Development____________________________

Rewarding____________________________________

Employee Retention______________________________

7.3 What impact do these involvement practices have on your attitude towards your organization?

____

____

7.4 Do you have any suggestions on current involvement practices in your organization? If you have, what suggestions will you make?

____

____

8 **Organizational performance**

By adopting strategic human resource management system in your organization, how much does organizational performance improve?

Changesinproductivity______________________________

Efficiency (hourly performance) ________________________

Skillperformance__________________________________

Turnover rate ____________________________________

9 **External environment Analysis**

Please provide example(s) about how the following factors influence strategic human resource management in your organizations (e.g. government policy, labour laws and regulation, unemployment, and technology development).

____

____

____

____

10 Future challenges

Given the radical changes in market and within organization, how will strategic human resource management system in your organization cope with these changes in future?

____

____

____

____

Appendix 3: Survey for Employees

A Study on SHRM/HPWS among Indigenous Chinese Companies

Questionnaire for Employees

Introduction

This questionnaire is divided into four main sections:

- The first section asks for general information about you and your organization.
- The second section asks about specific human resource policies and practices in your organization.
- The third section asks about the level of your participation in your organization.
- The last section asks about your job satisfaction and turnover intention.

There are no right or wrong answers. Please answer each question. Please be as accurate and honest as possible. All responses are held in the strictest confidence. We appreciate and thank you for your participation.

Section I – Interviewee Profile

The following questions are about some basic details of yourself.
Please write down your answers in the spaces provided.

1. Gender: ☐ Female ☐ Male

2. Age (on your last birthday): ______________________

3. Position (please specify): ______________________

4. What is your highest level of education: ______________________

5. How many years have you worked for this organization: ______________________

Section II – Implementation of HPWS

The following questions are about your awareness of HRM practices in your organization.

For each of the statements below, please indicate (√) the extent of your awareness or unawareness.

1= strongly unaware, 4 = neither aware nor unaware, and 7 = strongly aware

Are you aware that	*1*	*2*	*3*	*4*	*5*	*6*	*7*
1. Selective staffing							
1. Great effort is taken to select the right person.							
2. Long-term employee potential is emphasized.							
3. Considerable importance is placed on the staffing process.							
4. Very extensive efforts across departments are made in selection.							
2. Extensive training							
5. Extensive training programs are provided for employees.							
6. Employees will normally go through training programs every few years.							
7. There are formal training programs to teach new hires the skills they need to perform their job.							
8. Formal training programs are offered to employees in order to increase their promotability in this organization.							
3. Internal mobility							
9. Employees have few opportunities for upward mobility.							
10. Employees do not have any future in this organization.							
11. Promotion in this organization is based on seniority.							
12. Employees have clear career paths in this organization.							

Are you aware that	*1*	*2*	*3*	*4*	*5*	*6*	*7*
13. Employees who desire promotion have more than one potential position they could be promoted to.							
4. Employment security							
14. Employees in this job can be expected to stay with this organization for as long as they wish.							
15. Job security is almost guaranteed to employees in this job.							
5. Clear job description							
16. The duties in this job are clearly defined.							
17. This job has an up-to-date description.							
18. The job description for a position accurately describes all of the duties performed by individual employees.							
6. Results-oriented appraisal							
19. Performance is more often measured with objective quantifiable results.							
20. Performance appraisals are based on objective quantifiable results.							
21. Employee appraisals emphasize long term and group-based achievement.							
7. Incentive reward							
22. Employees in this job receive bonuses based on the profit of the organization.							
23. Close tie or matching of pay to individual/group performance.							
8. Participation							
24. Employees in this job are often asked by their supervisor to participate in decisions.							
25. Employees in this job are allowed to make decisions.							

Are you aware that	*1*	*2*	*3*	*4*	*5*	*6*	*7*
26. Employees are provided the opportunity to suggest improvements in the way things are done.							
27. Supervisors keep open communications with employees in this job.							

Section III – Trust in Management

The following questions are about your trust in management.

For each of the statements below, please indicate (√) the extent of your agreement or disagreement.

1 = strongly disagree, 4 = I neither agree nor disagree, and 7 = strongly agree.

I agree that	*1*	*2*	*3*	*4*	*5*	*6*	*7*
1. Ability							
1. My supervisor is very capable of performing his/her job.							
2. My supervisor is known to be successful at the things he/she tries to do.							
3. My supervisor has much knowledge about the work that needs done.							
4. I feel very confident about my supervisor's skills.							
5. My supervisor has specialized capabilities that can increase our performance.							
6. My supervisor is well qualified.							
2. Benevolence							
7. My supervisor is very concerned about my welfare.							
8. My needs and desires are very important to my supervisor.							
9. My supervisor would not knowingly do anything to hurt me.							
10. My supervisor really looks out for what is important to me.							

I agree that	*1*	*2*	*3*	*4*	*5*	*6*	*7*
11. My supervisor will go out of his/her way to help me.							
3. Integrity							
12. My supervisor has a strong sense of justice.							
13. I never have to wonder whether my supervisor will stick to its word.							
14. My supervisor tries hard to be fair in dealing with others.							
15. My supervisor's actions and behaviours are not very consistent.							
16. I like management's values.							
17. Sound principles seem to guide top management's behaviour.							

Section IV – Job Satisfaction

The following questions are about your level of satisfaction at work.

For each of the statements below, please indicate (√) the extent of your agreement or disagreement.

1 = strongly disagree, 4 = I neither agree nor disagree, and 7 = strongly agree.

I agree that	*1*	*2*	*3*	*4*	*5*	*6*	*7*
Job satisfaction							
1. I get support and guidance from my supervisor.							
2. Fringe benefits are distributed fairly in the firm.							
3. I have no anxiety about my job security.							
4. I have a chance for promotion.							
5. The person who performs highly has more chance to be promoted.							
6. I feel close to the people at work.							
7. I get personal growth and development I get in doing my job.							

I agree that	*1*	2	3	4	5	6	7
8. I am satisfied with my job for the time being.							
9. My job is a hobby to me.							
10. I am fairly paid for what I contribute to this firm.							
11. My pay is enough for me.							
12. My workload is quite fair.							

Section V – Turnover Intention

The following questions are about your intention of leaving current organization.

For each of the statements below, please indicate (√) the extent of your agreement or disagreement.

1 = strongly disagree, 4 = I neither agree nor disagree, and 7 = strongly agree.

I agree that	*1*	2	3	4	5	6	7
Turnover intention							
1. I intend to stay in this job for the foreseeable future.							
2. I will probably look for a new job within the next year.							
3. I do not intend to pursue alternate employment in the foreseeable future.							

THANK YOU VERY MUCH FOR YOUR TIME!

If you have any suggestions or additional comments, please feel free to drop us a line below.

Index

For Product Safety Concerns and Information please contact our EU
representative GPSR@taylorandfrancis.com
Taylor & Francis Verlag GmbH, Kaufingerstraße 24, 80331 München, Germany

www.ingramcontent.com/pod-product-compliance
Ingram Content Group UK Ltd.
Pitfield, Milton Keynes, MK11 3LW, UK
UKHW020947180425
457613UK00019B/574

* 9 7 8 0 3 6 7 3 7 4 6 9 3 *